NUTS AND BOLTS FOR THE SOCIAL SCIENCES

Nuts and Bolts
for the Social Sciences

JON ELSTER

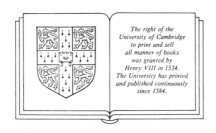

The right of the
University of Cambridge
to print and sell
all manner of books
was granted by
Henry VIII in 1534.
The University has printed
and published continuously
since 1584.

CAMBRIDGE UNIVERSITY PRESS

Cambridge

New York   Port Chester   Melbourne   Sydney

Published by the Press Syndicate of the University of Cambridge
The Pitt Building, Trumpington Street, Cambridge CB2 1RP
32 East 57th Street, New York, NY 10022, USA
10 Stamford Road, Oakleigh, Melbourne 3166, Australia

First published 1989

Printed in the United States of America

Library of Congress Cataloging-in-Publication Data
Elster, Jon, 1940–
Nuts and bolts for the social sciences / Jon Elster.
p.   cm.
Bibliography: p.
ISBN 0-521-37455-3.–ISBN 0-521-37606-8 (pbk.)
1. Social sciences – Methodology.   2. Social interaction.
I. Title.
H61.E434   1989   89-31449
300′.1 – dc20   CIP

British Library Cataloguing in Publication Data
Elster, Jon, *1940–*
Nuts and bolts for the social sciences.
1. Social sciences. Concepts
I. Title
300

ISBN 0-521-37455-3 hard covers
ISBN 0-521-37606-8 pbk

CONTENTS

v

PREFACE AND ACKNOWLEDGMENTS

MANY years ago I read about a book by a nineteenth-century German mathematician, Felix Klein, called *Elementary Mathematics from an Advanced Standpoint.* I never read it, but the title stuck in my mind. The present book could perhaps be subtitled *Elementary Social Science from an Advanced Standpoint.*

Or should it be the other way around – advanced social science from an elementary standpoint? In that case, my model would be a short and wonderful book by Richard Feynman, *QED,* an introduction to quantum electrodynamics for the general public. The comparison is not as presumptuous as one might think. On the one hand, Feynman's ability to go to the core of a subject, without technicalities but also without loss of rigor, may be unsurpassed in the history of science and is in any case beyond mine. On the other, quantum electrodynamics is more arcane than any of the topics discussed here. On balance, therefore, the reader may find my exposition just as intelligible.

The purpose of the book is reflected in its title: to introduce the reader to causal mechanisms that serve as the basic units of the social sciences. Though not a do-it-yourself kit, it might serve as a read-it-yourself kit for further study. The reader should be wary of the chapter on reinforcement, a topic about which I know little but which is too important to be neglected. I hope what I say is correct, but people who know more about it may find it superficial.

A word about style. I have tried to avoid flogging dead horses or belaboring the obvious; to be honest about the inevitable simplifications; to write simply and without jargon; to respect the reader's intelligence as well as his ignorance. I rely on examples, diagrams and nontechnical expositions, since, with one exception, I don't think more is needed. The exception is the chapter on bargaining, which stands in the same relation to current research as a child's drawing to a photograph. My hope is that the other chapters are like impressionistic paintings, in which light and shade make up for lack of focus.

The many footnotes serve several functions. Mainly, they are reminders that things are more complicated than the main text might suggest. They point to links between chapters that might otherwise not be noticed. Or they discuss paradoxes and curiosa of the sort that social scientists love, often to excess.

"Elster" in German is "magpie," someone who steals other people's silver. Since there are no references to or mention of other people's work in the book, it may read as if all the ideas in it are my own. The Bibliographical Essay is intended partly to dispel that impression, partly to serve as a guide to further studies.

Like some of my other books, this one began as lectures at the University of Chicago. I am indebted to my students for pushing me to the wall whenever they got the air of an ambiguity, inconsistency or downright error. I also thank George Ainslie, Ingrid Creppell, Stephen Holmes, Arthur Stinchcombe and Cass Sunstein for their comments on an earlier version.

Part One

INTRODUCTION

I

MECHANISMS

THE emphasis in this book is on *explanation by mechanisms*. It offers a toolbox of mechanisms – nuts and bolts, cogs and wheels – that can be used to explain quite complex social phenomena.

The social sciences, like other empirical sciences, try to explain two sorts of phenomena: events and facts. The election of George Bush as president is an event. The presence in the electorate of a majority of Republican voters is a fact, or a state of affairs. It is not immediately obvious what is more fundamental, events or facts. One might, quite plausibly, explain Bush's victory by the Republican majority. One might also, no less plausibly, explain the Republican majority as being the result of a series of events, each of which took the form of belief formation by an individual voter. The second perspective is the more fundamental: explaining events is logically prior to explaining facts. A fact is a temporal snapshot of a stream of events, or a pile of such snapshots. In the social sciences, the elementary events are individual human actions, including mental acts such as belief formation.

To explain an event is to give an account of why it happened. Usually, and always ultimately,[1] this takes the form of citing an earlier event as the cause of the event we want to explain, together with some account of the causal mechanism connecting the two events. Here is a simple, paradigmatic example. We want to know why someone changed his mind about a job he

1 Sometimes people explain events by citing other events that occur later rather than earlier in time. When valid, such explanations ultimately conform to the main pattern. The topic is further discussed in chapters VIII and IX.

3

previously held to be very desirable, but now finds utterly lacking in interest. The explanation has two elements. First, before changing his mind, he learned that he had no chances of getting the job. Second, there is a causal *mechanism,* often referred to as cognitive dissonance reduction, that makes people cease desiring what they cannot get, as in the story of the fox and the sour grapes. A more complex event might be a fall in average work tenure. The earlier event was legislation designed to enhance job security by requiring employers to give job tenure to all who had been employed for more than, say, two years. The causal mechanism is rational adaptation to the legislation by employers, who find it in their interest to dismiss workers just before the expiration of the two-year period.

Statements that purport to explain an event must be carefully distinguished from a number of other types of statement. First, causal explanations must be distinguished from true causal statements. To cite the cause is not enough: the causal mechanism must also be provided, or at least suggested. In everyday language, in most historical writings and in many social scientific analyses, the mechanism is not explicitly cited. Instead, it is suggested by the way in which the cause is described. Any given event can be described in many ways. In narrative explanations, it is tacitly presupposed that only causally relevant features of the event are used to identify it. If told that a person died as a result of having eaten rotten food, we assume that the mechanism was food poisoning. If told that he died as a result of eating food to which he was allergic, we assume that the mechanism was an allergic reaction. Suppose now that he actually died because of food poisoning, but that he was also allergic to the food in question, lobster. To say that he died because he ate food to which he had an allergy would be true, but misleading. It would suggest the wrong causal mechanism. To say that he died because he ate lobster would be true, but uninformative. It would suggest no causal mechanism at all and exclude very few. Indeed, the actual mechanism could be almost anything, from being hit by a car to being hit by a bullet, if either of these events was triggered by the person's eating lobster.

Second, causal explanations must be distinguished from assertions about correlation. Sometimes we are in a position to say that an event of a certain type is invariably or usually followed by an event of another kind. This does not allow us to say that events of the first type cause events of the second, because there is another possibility: the two might be common effects of a third event. Consider the finding that children in contested custody cases suffer more than children whose parents have reached a private custody agreement. It could be that the custody trial itself explains the difference, by causing pain and guilt in the children. It could also be, however, that custody disputes are more likely to occur when the parents are bitterly hostile toward each other and that children of such parents tend to be more unhappy. To distinguish between the two interpretations, we would have to measure suffering before and after the divorce.

Here is a more complex example, my favorite example, in fact, of this kind of ambiguity. In *Democracy in America*, Alexis de Tocqueville discusses the alleged causal connection between marrying for love and having an unhappy marriage. He points out that this connection obtains only in societies in which such marriages are the exception and arranged marriages are the rule. Only stubborn people will go against the current and two stubborn persons are not likely to have a very happy marriage.[2] In addition, people who go against the current are treated badly by their more conformist peers, inducing bitterness and more unhappiness. Of these arguments, the first rests on a noncausal correlation between marrying for love and unhappiness. The second does point to a true causal connection, albeit not the one that the critics of love marriages to whom Tocqueville addressed

2 Here the "third factor" is not an event, but a character trait: stubbornness. To explain the character trait, however, we would have to invoke (genetic and social) events. This illustrates the point, made earlier, that the priority of events over facts obtains ultimately, not immediately.

his argument had in mind. Marrying for love causes unhappiness only in a context where this practice is exceptional. Biologists often refer to such effects as "frequency dependent." I discuss this notion in chapter XI.

Third, causal explanations must be distinguished from assertions about necessitation. To explain an event is to give an account of why it happened *as* it happened. The fact that it might also have happened in some other way, and would have happened in some other way if it had not happened in the way it did, is neither here nor there. Consider a person who suffers from an incurable form of cancer, which is certain to kill him within one year. He is, however, killed in a car accident. To *explain* why he died within a certain time period, it is pointless to say that he *had to* die in that period because he had cancer. If all we know about the case is the onset of cancer, the limited life span of persons with that type of cancer and the death of the person, it is plausible to infer that he died because of the cancer. We have the earlier event and a causal mechanism sufficient to bring about the later event. But the mechanism is not necessary: it could be preempted by another. To find out what actually happened, we need more finely grained knowledge. The quest never ends: right up to the last second, something else could preempt the cancer. Yet the more we know, the more confident we are that we have the right explanation.[3]

The two problems we have just discussed add up to a weakness in the best-known theory of scientific explanation, that proposed by Carl Hempel. He argues that explanation amounts to logical deduction of the event to be explained, with general laws and statements of initial conditions as the premises. One objection is that the general laws might reflect correlation, not causation. Another is that the laws, even if genuinely causal,

---

3 Causal preemption should be distinguished from causal overdetermination. The latter is illustrated by a person being hit simultaneously by two bullets, each of which would have been sufficient to kill him. The former is illustrated by a person being hit by one bullet and as a result falling down, thereby avoiding being hit by another bullet, which would otherwise have killed him.

might be preempted by other mechanisms. This is why I have placed the emphasis here on mechanisms, not on laws. This is not a deep philosophical disagreement. A causal mechanism has a finite number of links. Each link will have to be described by a general law, and in that sense by a "black box" about whose internal gears and wheels we remain ignorant. Yet for practical purposes – the purposes of the working social scientist – the place of emphasis is important. By concentrating on mechanisms, one captures the dynamic aspect of scientific explanation: the urge to produce explanations of ever finer grain.

Fourth, causal explanations must be distinguished from storytelling. A genuine explanation accounts for what happened, as it happened. To tell a story is to account for what happened as it might have happened (and perhaps did happen). I have just argued that genuine explanations differ from accounts of what had to happen. I am now saying that they also differ from accounts of what may have happened. The point may seem trivial, or strange. Why would anyone want to come up with a purely conjectural account of an event? Is there any place in science for speculations of this sort. The answer is yes – but their place must not be confused with that of explanations.

Storytelling can suggest new, parsimonious explanations. Suppose that someone asserts that self-sacrificing or helping behavior is conclusive proof that not all action is self-interested or that emotional behavior is conclusive proof that not all action is rational.[4] One might conclude that there are three irreducibly different forms of behavior: rational and selfish, rational and nonselfish, and irrational. The drive for parsimony that characterizes good science should lead us to question this view.[5] Could it not be in one's self-interest to help others? Could it not be

---

4 A well-known example from another domain is provided by the numerous biologists who have asserted that living organisms cannot possibly be explained by chemical and physical theories.

5 Yet the sense for realism that also characterizes good science should make us wary of the simplistic tendency to believe that all reductionist attempts will succeed.

rational to be swayed by one's emotions? The first step toward finding a positive answer is telling a *plausible story* to show how these possibilities could be realized. It could be, for instance, that people help others because they expect reciprocation or that people become angry because that helps them to get their way. By telling a story one can transform an issue from a metaphysical one into one that is amenable to empirical research. The question now is whether the premises of the story are true, not whether it is possible or impossible to explain one range of phenomena in terms of other, less complex phenomena.

At the same time, storytelling can be harmful if it is mistaken for the real thing. Much of social science is driven by the idea that "everything has a function." Even behavior that appears to be harmful and maladaptive should be shown to be useful and, moreover, be explained in terms of its usefulness. To demonstrate function and usefulness, scholars often resort to storytelling. They have a considerable number of devices at their disposal. Behavior that isn't optimal now may have been so under other circumstances in the past. Behavior that isn't optimal taken in isolation may be a necessary ingredient in an optimal package solution. What is maladaptive for the individual may be good for society. With some ingenuity – and many scholars have a great deal – one can *always* tell a story in which things are turned upside down. But that doesn't prove they really are that way, any more than Kipling's *Just So Stories* explain how the leopard got its spots or the Ethiopian his color.

Finally, causal explanations must be distinguished from predictions. Sometimes we can explain without being able to predict, and sometimes predict without being able to explain. True, in many cases one and the same theory will enable us to do both, but I believe that in the social sciences this is the exception rather than the rule.

To see why we can have explanatory power without predictive power, consider once again the reduction of cognitive dissonance. In many people, this mechanism coexists with the exactly opposite one, captured in homely sayings such as "The grass is always greener on the other side of the fence" and "Forbidden fruit tastes best." Sometimes it seems as if people want to be unhappy, by desiring objects demonstrably out of reach simply because they are out of reach. Build a fence around someone, and he immediately wants to get out, while before he had no such thought in his mind. As far as I know, we have no theories that tell us when one or the other of these mechanisms will operate. When one of them does operate, we recognize it immediately, and so we can explain the behavior it generates. But we cannot reliably predict when it will operate.

Another example will help to bring the point home. When people try to make up their mind whether to participate in a cooperative venture, such as cleaning up litter from the lawn or voting in a national election, they often look to see what others are doing. Some of them will think as follows: "If most others cooperate, I too should do my share, but if they don't I have no obligation to do so." Others will reason in exactly the opposite way: "If most others cooperate, there is no need for me to do so. If few others cooperate, my obligation to do so will be stronger." In fact, most individuals are subject to both of these psychic mechanisms, and it is hard to tell before the fact which will dominate.

It is sometimes said that the opposite of a profound truth is another profound truth.[6] The social sciences offer a number of illustrations of this profound truth. They can isolate tendencies, propensities and mechanisms and show that they have implications for behavior that are often surprising and counterintuitive. What they are more rarely able to do is to state necessary and sufficient conditions under which the various mechanisms are switched on. This is another reason for emphasizing mechanisms rather than laws. Laws by their nature are general and do

6 "Opposite" must be taken in the sense of internal rather than external negation. The internal negation of "People prefer what they can have over what they cannot have" is "People prefer what they cannot have over what they can have." Both statements yield true and important insights. The external negation of the first statement is simply that "People do not prefer what they can have over what they cannot have," a statement that does not suggest any important insights.

not suffer exceptions. One cannot have a law to the effect that "if *p*, then sometimes *q*."[7] Mechanisms, by contrast, make no claim to generality. When we have identified a mechanism whereby *p* leads to *q*, knowledge has progressed because we have added a new item to our repertoire of ways in which things happen.

Conversely, we may have predictive power without explanatory power. To predict that less of a good will be bought when its price goes up, there is no need to form a hypothesis about consumer behavior. Whatever the springs of individual action – rational, traditional or simply random – we can predict that people will buy less of the good simply because they can afford less of it. Here there are several mechanisms that are constrained to lead to the same outcome, so that for predictive purposes there is no need to decide among them. Yet for explanatory purposes the mechanism is what matters. It provides understanding, whereas prediction at most offers control.[8]

Also, for predictive purposes the distinction among correlation, necessitation and explanation becomes pointless. If there is a lawlike regularity between one type of event and another, it does not matter whether it is due to a causal relation between them or to their being common effects of a third cause. In either case we can use the occurrence of the first type of event to predict the occurrence of the second. Nobody believes that the first symptoms of a deadly disease cause the later death, yet they are regularly used to predict that event. Similarly, it does not matter for predictive purposes whether a necessitating mechanism might be preempted by another. Knowing that a person has incurable cancer allows us to predict that he will die, whether or not he in fact dies from cancer.

7 Although Sidney Morgenbesser has suggested as the "first law of Jewish logic": if *p*, why not *q?*
8 "At most," for reasons discussed in chapter II.

10

Part Two

HUMAN ACTION

II

DESIRES AND OPPORTUNITIES

THE elementary unit of social life is the individual human action. To explain social institutions and social change is to show how they arise as the result of the action and interaction of individuals. This view, often referred to as methodological individualism, is in my view trivially true. Many think differently, however, and some of their arguments will be addressed in chapter XV. Here I want to stress that individual actions are themselves in need of explanation.[1]

A simple scheme for explaining an action is to see it as the end result of two successive filtering operations. We begin with a large set of all abstractly possible actions that an individual might undertake. The first filter is made up of all the physical, economic, legal and psychological *constraints* that the individual faces. The actions consistent with these constraints form his *opportunity set*. The second filter is a mechanism that determines which action within the opportunity set will actually be carried out. In this exposition the main mechanisms to be considered are rational choice (chapter III) and social norms (chapter XII).[2] Here I shall concentrate on choice-generated mechanisms, mainly for ease of exposition but also because I believe they are more fundamental than norm-generated ones.

1 The term "individual" will be used in an extended sense that also includes corporate decision makers, like firms or governments. (But see chapter XV.)
2 One might argue instead that social norms are among the constraints facing an individual. I find it more useful to think of constraints as creating a hard distinction between what is feasible and what is not. A person cannot outspend his income, suspend gravity or vote at times other than election days, but he can violate the norm against wearing brown shoes with evening dress or the norm of reciprocating favors.

13

In this perspective, actions are explained by opportunities and desires – by what people can do and by what they want to do. Consumer behavior is a simple example. If I go to a store with twenty dollars in my pocket and a firm intention to spend them (they will burn a hole in my pocket if I don't), there are only so many combinations of goods I can come out with. Which of these I actually end up buying depends on my wants, preferences, desires. Criminal behavior provides a more complex example. The effect of legal constraints is not to make criminal actions impossible, but to make them more costly. Without these constraints, riskless theft would be one of my opportunities. Given the constraints, my choice is between riskless law-abiding behavior and risky theft. It depends on the sure gains and possible losses associated with the alternatives and, since the gain from theft is immediate and certain while the loss is delayed and uncertain, on my time preferences (chapter V) and my attitude toward risk.[3]

Much social science consists of endlessly elaborate variations on the theme of opportunities and desires. I shall try to impose some structure on this bewildering variety of practices. This will also allow me to discuss some of the reasons – good and not so good – that people have adduced to argue that opportunities are more fundamental than preferences.

To begin with, we may note that we need not always appeal to both opportunities and preferences. Sometimes the constraints are so hard that there is no room left for the second filter to operate in. The opportunity set is reduced to a single action, in the explanation of which choices (or norms) have no role.[4] The rich and the poor alike have the opportunity to sleep under

---

3 In addition, internalized social norms might stop me from stealing even when there is no risk of detection and punishment.

4 There are schools of social theory, often referred to as "structuralist," which hold that all explanation of behavior takes this form. Marxists often argue, for instance, that workers are forced by circumstances to sell their labor to capitalists just as the latter are forced by competition to exploit workers. To see the flaw in the argument, it is sufficient to note that nobody is forced to be a capitalist: there is always the option of becoming a worker.

the bridges in Paris, but the poor may have no other opportunities.[5] Also, there are cases in which the nature of the second filter doesn't affect the outcome. As noted in chapter I, the fact that people (in the aggregate) buy less of a good when its price goes up can be explained independently of what motivates people (as individuals) to buy or not to buy. If their income remains the same, they will buy less of the good simply because they can afford less of it.

Scholars disagree on the relative importance of preferences and opportunities in explaining behavior. Some economists argue that all people have essentially the same preferences and desires: only opportunities differ. Although usually staunch defenders of rational-choice theory, they are led, paradoxically, to argue that choice almost doesn't matter because any variations in behavior must be explained by variations in opportunities. Most social scientists, however, believe that people differ in their desires as well as in their opportunities, and this view seems to me so obviously right as not to require further defense.

Yet in particular cases there is still room for debate. Historians of slavery, in classical antiquity or in the American South, have suggested two different explanations of the low rate of investment in these societies. Some have argued that the slaveowners lacked opportunities for investment. The slaves treated their tools so badly that investment in mechanized production was not a live option. Others have argued that the slaveowners lacked the motivation to invest, because they preferred a life of luxurious and conspicuous consumption. Similar debates are found in the sociology of education. Do children from working-class families drop out of school early because they cannot afford to go on or because their values differ from those of children with a middle-class background? These issues cannot be resolved on methodological grounds. They must be settled case

5 There may still be a nontrivial choice as to which bridge the poor shall sleep under. The point is quite general: the opportunity set rarely reduces to literally one physical option.

by case, by considering the empirical evidence. Yet they are often, but misleadingly, stated as methodological questions.

Opportunities are more basic than desires in one respect: they are easier to observe, not just by the social scientist but also by other individuals in society. In military strategy a basic dictum is that one should make one's plans on the basis of the opponent's (verifiable) capabilities, not on his (unverifiable) intentions. Often, this amounts to planning on a worst-case assumption: the opponent will hurt us if he can do so. If each side plans on the basis of the capabilities of the other side, and knows the other side to be doing the same, their actual preferences may not matter much.

Still another reason that opportunities might appear more fundamental than desires has to do with the possibility of influencing behavior. It is usually easier to change people's circumstances and opportunities than to change their minds.[6] This is a cost–benefit argument about the dollar effectiveness of alternative policies – not an argument about relative explanatory power. Even if the government has a good theory, which allows for both explanation and prediction, it may not allow for much control. The factors that are under government control are not always the causally important ones. Suppose that weak economic performance can be traced back to risk-averse businessmen and to strong labor unions. The government may be fully convinced that the mental attitude of managers is the more important cause and yet be unable to do anything about it. By contrast, unions can to some extent be controlled by income policies.

So far I have been arguing as if desires and opportunities are given independently of each other and can vary independently of each other. I now turn to cases in which both are influenced by a third factor, and then to cases in which they can influence each other directly (see Fig. II.1).

For illustrations of case A in Fig. II.1, I first turn to Tocque-

---

6 In addition, as argued later, the best way to change their minds may be to change their circumstances. But this is a separate argument.

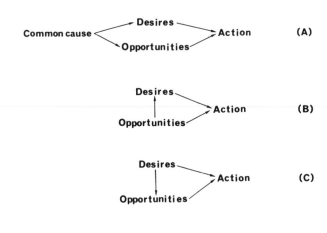

Figure II.1

ville. *Democracy in America* abounds with instances in which desires and opportunities are traced back to a common cause. Sometimes the two act in concert. Thus, Tocqueville says, slavery not only prevents white men from making their fortune, but even diverts them from wishing to do so. In America, the voters never elect men of distinction to public office, partly because they have no opportunity to do so (men of distinction do not want to go into politics) and partly because they would not desire to elect superior candidates were they to appear. In other cases, Tocqueville argues, the effect on desires and the effect on opportunities work in opposite directions. There is no time in their life, he claims, at which Americans have both the leisure and the inclination to study, whence the absence of well-educated Americans. In America, religion – itself an effect of democracy – removes the desire to do what democracy allows people to do.

There is a saying that necessity is the mother of invention. Similarly, social historians often take it for given that hardship is the mother of revolt and other forms of collective action. Neither claim is obviously valid. What is true is that when people are

17

badly off their motivation to innovate or to rebel is high. Their capacity or opportunity to do so, however, is the lowest when they are in tight circumstances. Innovation requires resources, time, costly investments with a delayed and uncertain payoff – but this is exactly what firms on the brink of bankruptcy cannot afford. Prosperous firms can afford to innovate – but they may not bother to do so. Participation in collective action requires the ability to take time off from directly productive activities – but this is exactly what the impoverished worker or peasant cannot afford. The middle peasant and the worker who has managed to save a bit can afford to join a rebellion or a strike, but their motivation is less acute. Since actual innovation and actual participation depend on both desires and opportunities, and since these vary in opposite directions with hardship of circumstances, we cannot tell *a priori* which level of hardship is most likely to favor the effect in question. Marx argued that civilization arose in the temperate zones because only there did the need for improvement meet with opportunities for improvement. Where Nature is too lavish there is no need, and where she is too scanty there are no opportunities.

Desires and opportunities may also affect each other directly. Consider first the mechanism indicated by case B in Fig. II.1. Chapter I touched on some ways in which opportunities can affect desires: people may end up desiring most what they can get.[7] Again we may quote Tocqueville on slavery: "Is it a blessing of God, or a last malediction, this disposition of the soul that gives men a sort of depraved taste for the cause of their afflictions?" This would provide a further reason for thinking opportunities more basic than preferences. Opportunities and desires jointly are the proximate causes of action, but at a further remove only opportunities matter since they also shape desires. This way of stating the matter is too strong, however. The "sour grapes" mechanism ensures that there is no option outside the opportunity set that is preferred to the most preferred option

7 Or, more perversely, what they cannot get.

within it, but it does not cause any particular feasible option to be the most preferred.

The opposite mechanism, that of case C in Fig. II.1, can also operate. Sometimes the opportunity set is deliberately shaped by a person's desires. I do not have in mind here the practically important but theoretically trivial desire to expand one's opportunity set, but the more puzzling cases in which people find it in their interest to reduce the set of options available to them. I shall discuss two reasons people might engage in such self-limiting or self-binding behavior.

First, there is weakness of will. I discuss this phenomenon at more length in chapters IV and V, but it is also relevant here. As illustrated by the story of Ulysses and the sirens, people do not always trust themselves to behave rationally. If they can anticipate the kind of situations in which they might lose their head, they can act strategically to prevent the opportunity for doing so from arising. I may decide not to go to the office party if I am afraid I will do something foolish. On January 1, I may ask my dentist to bill me in full if on January 20 I cancel my appointment for January 21. A government might hand over control of financial policy to the International Monetary Fund to prevent itself from giving in to popular demands for wage increases.

Next, there is strategic interaction. One can sometimes improve one's outcome by eliminating certain options from the opportunity set. To see how, consider a game between two agents or players, I and II (Fig. II.2). In this game, I moves first. He can either terminate the game by moving left, in which case both get a reward of 3, or move right, in which case II has the next move. In that case, II can ensure 2 for himself and 4 for I by moving left, whereas if he moves right both get 1. Clearly, if II is rational, he will move left. Similarly, if I is rational and knows that he can count on II's rationality, he will move right. Note, however, that the outcome (4, 2) is not what II would most prefer. He would rather that I move left to the outcome (3, 3). One way in which II can achieve this goal is to *eliminate his option of going left* at the second

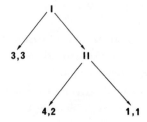

Figure II.2

stage. In that case, I will know that the outcome of going right will be (1, 1). To avoid that, he goes left instead. More concretely, suppose that I and II are two opposing armies. I's first move corresponds to the choice between opening negotiations and attacking. If I chooses to attack, II then has the choice between retreating and fighting. Because a war would be so destructive, it would then be in II's interest to retreat. However, II may use the classical stratagem of burning his bridges, thus making retreat physically impossible and, as a consequence, bringing I to the negotiation table.[8]

Strictly speaking, there is something incongruous about explaining an action in terms of opportunities and desires. Opportunities are objective, external to a person. Desires are subjective and internal. We have no problem in understanding how external objects can act upon each other to produce an outcome, nor in grasping the notion of purely psychic causality. It is less clear how objective and subjective elements can interact to produce an action. In fact, what explains the action is the person's desires together with his *beliefs* about the opportunities. Because beliefs can be mistaken, the distinction is not trivial. The person may fail to be aware of certain opportunities and therefore not choose the best available means of realizing his desire. Conversely, if he wrongly believes certain unfeasible options to be feasible, the action may have disastrous results. It would be

8 Player II might also burn his bridges if he anticipates that weakness of will may prevent him from fighting if he has another way out.

naive to think, for instance, that public policy can be explained by the goals of government and the opportunities that, objectively speaking, are open to it. Rather, goals interact with beliefs – in fact, highly controversial theories – about what are feasible economic policies.

III

RATIONAL CHOICE

WHEN faced with several courses of action, people usually do what they believe is likely to have the best overall outcome. This deceptively simple sentence summarizes the theory of rational choice. In this chapter (and the next) I attempt to convey the flavor of the complexities hidden behind this formulation.

Rational choice is instrumental: it is guided by the outcome of action. Actions are valued and chosen not for themselves, but as more or less efficient means to a further end.[1] A simple example is the entrepreneur who wants to maximize profit. To achieve this end, he carefully considers which products to offer, how much of them to produce and how to produce them. A more complex example is the general who has been told to defeat the enemy army at any cost to himself. Before he can deploy his troops, he must form an opinion of the enemy's plans. In addition, he must take steps to give the enemy a wrong idea about his own plans. Since he knows that the enemy generals are aware of these calculations, and are in fact going through similar reasoning themselves, he must try to outguess and outsmart them. A more controversial example is that of the artist who is experimenting with different sketches until he "gets it right." He is considering alternative means to the same end, the creation of a work that has aesthetic value, rejecting most of them and finally accepting one.

Sometimes the distinction between means and end seems

---

1 By contrast, behavior guided by social norms is not concerned with outcomes. This contrast is explored in chapter XIII.

pointless. If, when offered the choice between an orange and an apple, I take the orange, it is not because of any outcome that I want to bring about. It is not as if I take the orange to create a certain sensation in my taste buds.[2] I take it because I would rather have an orange than an apple. When I decide that I would rather spend time with a friend than stay late at the office, there need not be any common goal to which both actions are alternative means. It is, let us assume, simply more important to me to be with my friend than to finish my work. Although these choices do not fall into the means-to-an-end category, this is no reason for saying they are not rational.

There is a way, however, by which such choices can be assimilated to instrumental action. By asking the individual, or by observing his behavior, we can find out how he ranks the options.[3] A person might prefer three oranges to four apples, but choose five apples over three oranges. A list of such pairwise comparisons is called the person's *preference ordering*. Using a mathematical trick, the preference ordering can be converted into a *utility function*, which is a way of assigning numbers to options so that the more preferred options receive higher numbers.[4] We can then say that the person acts so as to maximize utility, as long as we keep in mind that this is nothing but a convenient way of saying that he does what he most prefers. There is no implication of hedonism. In fact, his preferred op-

---

2 However, my choice of the orange obviously has *something* to do with taste sensations, as we shall see in chapter IX.

3 These may be options within his opportunity set, or outside it.

4 This step from preferences to utility functions is possible only if the preferences are "well behaved." Three conditions must be fulfilled. (1) The person must be able to compare any two options with each other. He must prefer the one, or prefer the other, or think them equally good. (2) The person must be consistent in his preferences: if he prefers an orange to an apple and an apple to a pear, he must also prefer the orange to the pear. (3) The person must be able to trade off values against each other. To explain this condition, it is easiest to use an example violating it: a voter who ranks the candidates solely according to their views on tax policy except when they happen to have the same position on that issue, in which case he ranks them according to their views on disarmament.

tion might be one that gives pleasure to others and none to himself.[5]

Concern with outcomes can be self-defeating. Although rational action is instrumental, some forms of instrumental action are downright irrational. Insomnia, impotence and stuttering get worse if one tries to do something about them. They are more likely to go away if one ceases to think about them – but that is not something that can be the outcome of an action. Spontaneity will elude us if we try to behave spontaneously. We cannot believe at will or forget at will, at least not in the sense in which one can raise one's arm at will. We cannot tickle ourselves, surprise ourselves or deliberately fool ourselves, much as we might wish to. We may wish to be esteemed and admired by others, but actions that we or others undertake for the sole purpose of achieving this end will undermine themselves. An important policy example is that of job creation for the purpose of enhancing people's self-esteem. It is true that having a regular job is an important source of self-esteem, but only on the condition that the main point of the job is to produce a good or service that consumers or taxpayers value sufficiently to pay for. Self-esteem is essentially a byproduct of actions undertaken for other ends – it cannot be the sole purpose of policy. Or take Tocqueville's view that the main value of political democracy is that it generates restless activity and superabundant energy in society and thereby makes it more prosperous. While possibly true, the assertion could not be a sufficient argument for introducing democratic institutions. For democracy to have prosperity as a byproduct, it must first be taken seriously as a form of government.

Rational choice is concerned with finding the *best* means to given ends. It is a way of adapting optimally to the circumstances. Optimal adaptation can also be brought about by mechanisms other than rational choice. These are considered in chapters VIII and IX. Here we should note that rational choice is not an infalli-

5 I say more about this in chapter VI.

ble mechanism, since the rational person can choose only what he *believes* to be the best means. As explained at the end of chapter II, this belief may well be erroneous. He may miss some opportunities, or stumble by mistake. Not only is it human to err: it may even be rational to do so, if all the evidence happens to point in the wrong direction. In the next chapter I discuss some ways in which belief formation can fail to be rational. Here my point is simply that the process can be rational and yet fail to reach the truth. Truth is a relation between a belief and what the belief is about. When Othello believes that Desdemona is deceiving him and she isn't, he is entertaining a false belief. By contrast, rationality is a relation between a belief and the grounds on which it is held. In light of the evidence presented to him by Iago, Othello's belief might well be rational.

Yet this example suggests the need to go further, because we do not really think that Othello's belief was rational. At the very least, he should have found out more about what Desdemona had done. More generally, we must require not only that beliefs be rational with respect to the available evidence, but also that the amount of evidence collected be in some sense optimal. On the one hand, there is a risk of collecting too little evidence. The doctor must examine his patient before he operates, lest he cut in the wrong place. On the other hand, there is a risk of collecting too much evidence. If the doctor's examination is too exhaustive, the patient may die. Let me elaborate on the second of these dangers.

Other things being equal, a decision is likely to be better the more evidence we gather and the longer we deliberate, but other things are not always equal. By the time we have reached a decision, the occasion to act may have passed us by. The patient may be dead, the firm gone into bankruptcy or the battle lost. Less dramatically, the costs of deliberating may exceed the benefits. Contested child custody cases provide a good illustration. In most Western countries today these are decided by the "best interests of the child"; that is, custody is given to the parent whom the court finds most fit to take care of the child.

This principle requires fine-tuned, protracted comparisons between the parents to decide who is best suited. In the end, let us assume, the fitter parent is selected. Yet custody litigation imposes great emotional damage on the child, arguably more than what would result if custody were given to the less fit parent. One should ask whether it is in the best interest of the child to let custody follow the best interests of the child. The decision that would have been best if found instantaneously and costlessly may not, all things considered, be the best if costs of decision making are taken into account.[6]

The place of belief in rational choice requires a more careful discussion. So far, I have argued as if beliefs are a matter of black or white: either we believe that something is the case, or we believe that it isn't.[7] Often we do make up our minds in this way; and often it would be pedantic to do otherwise. Yet in principle, all factual beliefs are a matter of probabilities. For all practical purposes, I can count on not being hit by a meteor while writing this chapter, and yet there is a small chance that it could happen. In many choice situations probabilities have to be taken very seriously. When choosing among crops, farmers have to consider the likelihood of early frost in the fall, of too little rain in the spring and of too much in the summer. Often they hedge their bets, by choosing a crop that leaves them reasonably well off regardless of the weather.

A numerical example may help. There are two crops, A and B, and two possible states of the weather, Good and Bad, assumed to be equally likely. The income from the crops under the two conditions are given in the following tabulation. Numbers in parentheses indicate the utility a farmer derives from the various income levels. They are chosen to reflect the nearly

6 In child custody cases, protracted fact finding can also modify what *is* the child's interest. Since courts place great emphasis on the continuity of the child–parent relationship, there is a presumption, which grows stronger as the case drags on, in favor of the parent who has temporary custody.

7 This must not be confused with the following logical truth. Either we believe that something is the case, or we don't believe it (the distinction between internal and external negation).

universal tendency for each extra dollar of income to give ever smaller increments in utility (the principle of decreasing marginal utility).[8]

Weather	A ($)	B ($)
Bad	10,000 (10)	15,000 (36)
Good	30,000 (60)	20,000 (50)
Average	20,000 (50)	17,500 (45)

In the long run, the farmer will earn more with crop A than crop B, since it has a higher average yield. In bad years, however, he will be worse off with A than with B. For that reason he will prefer B over A.[9] If crop A is chosen, the average income is $20,000 with a corresponding utility level of 50. Average utility is 35. Correspondingly, the utility of the average income from crop B is 45, while the average utility is 43. The average income (and hence the utility of the average income) is higher with A. There is no year, however, in which the average income and corresponding utility level are realized. The farmer cannot live off his average income,[10] anymore than he can have an average family of 2.2 children. What counts is the average of the realized utility levels.[11] Since average utility is higher with B, this crop will be chosen.

8 Intellectual honesty requires me to signal that the concept of utility employed here is less innocent than what I referred to earlier as "nothing but" the expression of preferences. The scope of the present exposition prevents me from going into detail.

9 Thus there is no need to stipulate peasant conservatism to explain the resistance to some of the high-yield crops introduced by the Green Revolution. If these crops also had higher variance, the resistance might have been perfectly rational.

10 He could do that, of course, if he saved in the good years.

11 The reader might justifiably ask whether *risk aversion* could not lead the farmer also to take account of the difference between the utility levels in good and bad years. Because the notion of utility used here is defined in a way that already incorporates attitudes toward risk, this proposal would, however, involve double counting.

The theory of decision making under risk tells people to maximize *expected utility*. In cases like the one I have just discussed, this means the same as utility averaged over many periods. The theory has been extended, however, to cover choice situations that do not repeat themselves day after day or year after year. In that case the decision maker is asked to rely on his "subjective probabilities" or, in less solemn language, on his informed hunches. The utility of each possible outcome of an action is weighted by the estimated probability of that outcome, to yield the expected utility of the action. The theory tells us to take the action that has associated with it the highest expected utility. In the next chapter I state my reasons for being skeptical about this extension of the theory.

To act rationally is to do as well for oneself as one can. When two or more rational individuals interact, they may do much worse for themselves than they could have done. This insight is perhaps the main practical achievement of *game theory*, or the theory of interdependent decisions. But the theory is also useful in a number of other ways. In fact, once one has come to appreciate it fully, it appears not to be a theory in the ordinary sense, but the natural, indispensable framework for understanding human interaction. It is, in that respect, more akin to logic than to an empirical discipline. It becomes an empirical theory once we add principles of behavior that can be tested and found to be true or false, but it does not stand or fall with empirical testing.

The basic principles of game theory are illustrated by the game in Fig. II.2. The ingredients in this example are common to all games. There are two or more *players*. Each of them has the choice between two or more *strategies*. Each set of choices generates a set of *rewards*. The reward of each player depends on the choices made by all others, not only on his own decision. The players are assumed to make their choices *independently* of each other, in the sense that they cannot make binding agreements to coordinate their decisions. In another sense, however, the choices are interdependent, because each has to make his decision on the basis of his anticipation of what the other(s) will do. In the game of Fig. II.2, player I has to put himself in the position of II before he can make his decision. Conversely, II's decision to burn his bridges would turn on his analysis of what I would do if forced to choose between negotiating and fighting.

In the best known of all games, the Prisoner's Dilemma,[12] both players have a *dominant strategy,* that is, a strategy that is the best reply to all moves by the opponent:

	b_1	b_2
a_1	3, 3	1, 4
a_2	4, 1	2, 2

Call a_1 and b_1 cooperative strategies and a_2 and b_2 noncooperative strategies. We see that for each player noncooperation dominates cooperation. A rational player will choose the noncooperative strategy, fully knowing that the other will do the same and that the outcome brought about by their action will be *worse for both* than what they could have achieved by cooperating. Chapter XIII is devoted to further discussion of this dilemma, which is omnipresent in social life. Here I simply want to warn against the temptation to argue that, since the players knowingly do worse for themselves than they could have done, they cannot *really* be rational. If the two players acted as one, this argument would be correct, but since they don't it is invalid. The notion of rational choice is defined for an individual, not for a collectivity of two or more individuals. If an individual has an option that is superior to his other options regardless of what other people do, he would be irrational not to take it. The fact that all would benefit if all acted irrationally is neither here nor there.

12 The dilemma derives its name from the following anecdote (with payoff numbers inserted). Two prisoners, suspected of having collaborated on a crime, are placed in separate cells. The police tell each of them that he will be released (4) if he denounces the other and the other does not denounce him. If they both denounce each other, both will get three years imprisonment (2). If he does not denounce the other, but the other denounces him, he will get five years (1). If neither denounces the other, the police have sufficient evidence to send each to prison for one year (3).

IV

WHEN RATIONALITY FAILS

RATIONAL-CHOICE theory aims at explaining human behavior. To achieve this, it must, in any given case, proceed in two steps. The first step is to determine what a rational person would do in the circumstances. The second step is to ascertain whether this is what the person actually did. If the person did what the theory predicted he would do, it can add the case to its credit side.[1] Similarly, the theory can fail at each of the two steps. First, it can fail to yield determinate predictions. Second, people can fail to conform to its predictions – they can behave irrationally.

To explain how these problems arise, let me first summarize the main argument of chapter III. An action, to be rational, must be the final result of three optimal decisions. First, it must be the best means of realizing a person's desire, given his beliefs. Next, these beliefs must themselves be optimal, given the evidence available to him. Finally, the person must collect an optimal amount of evidence – neither too much nor too little. That amount depends both on his desires – on the importance he attaches to the decision – and on his beliefs about the costs and benefits of gathering more information. The whole process, then, can be visualized as depicted in Fig. IV.1.

Here desires are the only independent element, to which all others are subservient. As David Hume wrote, "Reason is, and ought only to be, the slave of the passions." He did not mean, I

---

1 The correct explanation may still, as we know from chapter I, be a different one. Rational choice may be preempted by another mechanism. Or the person, although not rational, might by accident do what rationality would require him to.

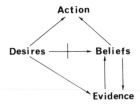

Figure IV.1

am sure, that reason should yield to every whim of the passions. In particular, he would not have legislated the power of the passions to act directly on one's beliefs, as in wishful thinking. (In the figure, this is indicated by a blocked arrow.)[2] As the French historian Paul Veyne has put it, beliefs born of passion serve passion badly; for slaves to serve their master well, they must have some degree of independence and autonomy of execution.

Before we proceed, let us look more closely at Hume's statement. It implies that the notion of *rational desires* is meaningless. Reason cannot dictate to the passions what their objects should be. Hume would certainly have conceded that reason can be helpful in eliminating logically incoherent desires, such as wanting to have one's cake and eat it too, but otherwise the passions are not subject to rational assessment. One may dislike a desire, perhaps think it immoral, but it makes no sense to decry it as irrational. This view is also the dominant one in contemporary social science. For most economists, in particular, desires and preferences are just like tastes, and "de gustibus non est disputandum." Later, I shall question this view.

First, I shall explain how rational-choice theory can fail through indeterminacy. In general, there are two forms of indeterminacy. There may be *several* actions that are equally and optimally good. Or there may be *no* action that is at least as good as all others.

Consider first indeterminacy of action, given one's beliefs and

2 We shall see that some effects of desires on the evidence-collecting process are illegitimate for similar reasons.

31

desires. Multiple optima often arise. I am trivially indifferent between two identical cans of Campbell's soup in the supermarket. I want one of them, but it doesn't matter which. Less trivially, a manager might maximize profits in two different ways: by a low volume of sales with high profits per sale or a high volume with low profits per sale. What he does might be very important for the workers who will be laid off if he chooses the low-volume option, but if profit is all he cares about we will not be able to explain why he chooses one rather than the other option. Yet such cases arise only by accident. It can easily happen that a person is indifferent between two qualitatively different options, but only by accident that these are also top-ranked in the opportunity set. There are no choice situations in which multiple optima tend to arise *systematically*.[3]

Cases in which, for given beliefs and desires, there is no optimal action arise when people are unable to compare and rank all the options.[4] If there are several actions than which none is better, I may be unable to say which of them I prefer *and also unable to say they are equally good*. This is incommensurability, not indifference. A simple test allows us to distinguish between the two. Assume that, for two options x and y, I have no preference for either. If I am indifferent between them, I should always prefer x together with an extra dollar over y. If however, I do not prefer x-plus-a-dollar over y, it shows that x and y are incommensurable.

Important decisions often involve incommensurable options. The choice, say, between going to law school or to a school of forestry, assuming that both attract me strongly, is a choice of career and life style. If I had tried both for a lifetime, I might be able to make an informed choice between them. As it is, I know

---

3 An exception is equilibrium behavior with random choice of strategy. This topic is discussed in chapter XI.

4 They can also arise in bizarre cases, like the following. I am told that, if I write down a positive number (strictly larger than zero), I will get a dollar reward equal to 1 divided by that number. Clearly, for any number I write down there is a smaller number that would give me a greater reward.

too little about them to make a rational decision. What often happens in such cases is that peripheral considerations move to the center. In my ignorance about the first decimal – whether my life will go better as a lawyer or as a forester – I look to the second decimal. Perhaps I opt for law school because that will make it easier for me to visit my parents on weekends.[5] This way of deciding is as good as any – but it is not one that can be underwritten by rational-choice theory as superior to, say, simply tossing a coin.

Beliefs are indeterminate when the evidence is insufficient to justify a judgment about the likelihood of the various outcomes of action. This can happen in two main ways: through uncertainty, especially about the future, and through strategic interaction.

Consider a firm's decision about how much to invest in research and development. To decide rationally, the firm must estimate the probable outcome of the investment – how likely it is that its innovative activities will lead to a profitable innovation – as well as the investments made by other firms and the probable outcome of those investments. Now the outcome of innovative activities is inherently uncertain. The firm cannot foresee with any precision whether it will hit the jackpot or come out with empty hands. Against the background of a constantly changing technology, past records are not good predictors of future success.

Even if the firm could estimate the chances of making a profitable innovation, it could not be certain of hitting upon it before other firms did. Under winner-take-all conditions, this is crucial. The more a firm invests in research and development, the greater are its chances of getting there first.[6] If other firms invest a large amount, our firm has a poor chance of winning. The

---

5 Even though I cannot compare x and y, I have no difficulty comparing one dollar with no dollars.

6 This statement holds true even if uncertainty about the future prevents us from saying anything about *how great* the chances are at various levels of investment.

rational decision might well be not to invest at all. Other firms, however, are presumably going through the same calculations. If they all decide to invest little, our firm should invest heavily. But, once again, this reasoning applies equally to the other firms, and if they all invest heavily, our firm should drop out. We are going in circles: each firm should invest much if and only if the others invest little. There is no basis here for rational belief formation, and hence no firm basis for action.[7] To explain investment decisions we might do better to follow Keynes and invoke the "animal spirits" of entrepreneurs.

There are some – they are called Bayesian decision theorists – who would disagree with what I have just said. They argue that, since we always have *some* knowledge about the choice situation, it must be better to use it to form subjective probability estimates than not to use it at all. The argument is seductive, but I don't think it is valid. Although we know much about the conflict in the Persian Gulf, there is no way in which we can piece together our information to come up with a reliable subjective probability of a war breaking out between Iran and the United States within the next six months.[8] Knowledge about the second decimal in a number is, taken by itself, strictly useless.

This is not to deny that such probabilities can be elicited – only to deny that they are reliable and that it is rational to use them as a basis for action. We can offer a person a choice between two bets. One bet says that if there is a war he will get a thousand dollars, otherwise nothing. The other bet says that he will get a thousand dollars with a probability of p percent and nothing with a probability of $100 - p$ percent. The value of p for which he is indifferent between the two bets is the subjective probability he attaches to the war. It turns out, however, that

7 This is not quite true. There is an equilibrium in which all firms use a random-izing device to decide how much to spend on research and development. The problem, as explained in chapter XI, is that the equilibrium is highly unstable. Empirically, we do not observe firms using lottery wheels or dice to make their investment decisions.

8 Time of writing: October 1987.

this value depends heavily on the procedure used for eliciting it. If we begin with a low value of p and move upward, the value is much lower than it would be if we began with a high value of p and moved downward. Yet if we are truly measuring something in the person's mind, the result should not depend on the method of measurement. Since it does, the probability is an artifact of the procedure.

Deciding how much evidence to collect can be tricky. If the situation is highly stereotyped, as a medical diagnosis is, we know pretty well the costs and benefits of additional information.[9] In situations that are unique, novel and urgent, like fighting a battle or helping the victim of a car accident, both costs and benefits are highly uncertain. There is a risk of acting too soon, on too little information – and a risk of delaying until it is too late. If we knew more, we could tell which risk was the larger – but we have no grounds for rationally deciding whether to risk acquiring that knowledge. Thus we just have to act, more or less arbitrarily. In between these two extremes fall most choice situations of everyday life. If I am out to gather mushrooms, I know I should spend some time looking for a good place and also that it would be pointless to go on looking until it got dark. I should look for a while, and then stop looking and begin gathering, where "a while" could be anything between ten minutes and a couple of hours. Within this range, there is indeterminacy. Since I cannot hope to make an optimal decision, I will have to do with one that is "good enough."

When rational choice is indeterminate, some other mechanism must take up the slack. That could be the principle of "satisficing," of choosing something that is good enough. The explanatory burden is then shifted to the notion of an aspiration

9 "To detect intestinal cancer, it has become common to perform a series of six inexpensive simple tests. . . . The benefits of the first two tests are significant. However, when calculations are done for each of the last four tests to determine the cost of detecting a case of cancer (not even curing it), the costs are discovered to be \$49,150, \$469,534, \$4,724,695, and \$47,107,214, respectively" (P. Menzel, *Medical Costs, Moral Choices*, New Haven, Conn.: Yale University Press, 1983, p. 6).

level, which determines what counts as good enough. Until more is known about why people's aspiration levels differ, the theory of satisficing remains unsatisfactory.[10] More generally, we do not have a theory of what people do when they would like to act rationally but rational choice is indeterminate. One thing they sometimes do is to deny the indeterminacy. Human beings have a very strong desire to have reasons for what they do and find indeterminacy hard to accept. They tend to shy away from decision procedures suggested by indeterminacy, such as making up one's mind by the toss of a coin. Instead, they may put their trust in fictitious subjective probabilities. Or as in the child custody case discussed in chapter III, they go on until they find the decision that would have been optimal if found instantaneously and costlessly. Or they decide on the basis of the second decimal, although ignorant about the first. These practices represent an irrational belief in the power of rationality. The first task of a theory of rational choice is to be clear about its own limits. Sometimes, as Pascal said, nothing is more rational than the abdication of reason.

Other forms of irrationality can be located at various levels in Fig. IV.1. Sometimes people fail to choose what they believe to be the best means to realize their desires. If it happens by mistake – by pushing the wrong button – it is not irrational. If they knowingly and deliberately act against their desires, it is. Suppose I am offered a cigarette when I am trying to quit smoking. On balance, my desires tell me to refuse, and yet I may accept. The culprit here is weakness of will, the vulnerability to desires that I myself acknowledge as weaker than the desires that point in the opposite direction. When the weaker desires win out, it must be because they are in some sense stronger – not stronger as reasons, but stronger as sheer psychic turbulence. In the next chapter I discuss a special case of weakness of will that is caused by the greater immediacy of the present and

10 The slack could also be taken up by something like social norms, to be discussed in chapter XIII. There, however, I consider social norms as an alternative to rational choice, not as a mere supplement to it.

the correspondingly smaller efficacy of the future. But weakness of will can take many other forms. I may yield to selfishness when I believe the claims of other people are really stronger. Conversely, I may think, on some given occasion, that my present-oriented or selfish concerns outweigh the claims of the future or of other people, and yet be unable to give myself a break. Compulsive hoarding can be just as weak-willed as impulsive spending.[11]

Irrational behavior can also stem from irrational beliefs. Most conspicuously, beliefs can be subverted by the passions they are supposed to serve. Wishful thinking – the tendency to believe that the facts are as one would like them to be – is a pervasive phenomenon, the importance of which in human affairs can hardly be overstated. Freud explained it in terms of the "pleasure principle," the mind's tendency to seek immediate gratification.[12] I feel better if I believe things are as I would like them to be, even though I would ultimately be better served by believing them to be as they in fact are.[13] Wishful thinking can operate directly, through the blocked arrow in Fig. IV.1, or indirectly, through the gathering of evidence. The latter, subtler mechanism operates as follows. Initially, let us assume, the evidence does not support the belief that I would like to be true. I then proceed to collect more evidence, adjusting and updating my beliefs as I go along. If at some point the sum total of the

11 Here is a more complicated example: I wish that I didn't wish that I didn't wish to eat cream cake. I wish to eat cream cake because I like it. I wish that I didn't like it, because, as a moderately vain person, I think it is more important to remain slim. But I wish I was less vain. (But do I think that only when I wish to eat cake?)

12 It is not a question of deliberately adopting the belief that the facts are as I would like them to be. As I said in chapter III, one cannot decide to believe, any more than one can decide to forget. Rather, the mechanism operates unconsciously, "behind my back."

13 This does not explain the tendency of the ingrained pessimist to believe that things are as he would like them *not* to be. An analogue of this perverse mechanism is the tendency, mentioned in chapter I, to desire what one cannot get, just because one cannot get it. I do not know of any satisfactory explanation of these self-destructive propensities.

evidence collected so far supports my preferred belief, I stop. I can then truly tell myself and others that my belief is supported by the available evidence, unlike crude wishful thinking, which simply goes in the face of the evidence.[14]

Wishful thinking, although undesirable in itself, sometimes goes together with other things that we would not wish to lose. A depressing finding from social psychology is that the individuals who have the best judgment – who are most able, that is, to be guided by the reality principle rather than the pleasure principle – are clinically depressed people. They are sadder, but wiser. Conversely, people in a normal hedonic state – who are neither manic nor depressed – tend to overestimate their abilities and to believe that other people think more highly of them than they in fact do. If we are to achieve anything at all, we must believe we can do more than we in fact can. A degree of irrational, wishful thinking is the price we pay for the motivation to go on with the business of living. Although our passions may be badly served by the beliefs they generate, *we* are better served by caring so much for some things that we lose our heads about them. I have more to say about the emotions in chapter VII.

Belief formation can also go wrong without any nudging from the passions. Especially when dealing with statistical matters, our minds are subject to cognitive illusions and fallacies that have been charted in fascinating detail over the past ten or fifteen years. Many were first demonstrated in experiments and later recognized in real-life situations. A common error is to attach excessive importance to personal experience and current events, at the expense of impersonal sources and past events. Stock prices, for instance, are excessively influenced by the current performance of firms and insufficiently by their past records. In the 1972 presidential campaign, trained reporters predicted that McGovern could not lose by more than ten points.

---

14 In Fig. IV.1 there should be, therefore, a blocked arrow from desires to evidence, in addition to the arrow indicating the justified influence of desires on the decision about how much evidence to collect.

They knew he was trailing by twenty points in the polls and that in twenty-four years not a single major poll had been wrong by more than 3 percent, but the wildly enthusiastic crowds they had seen with their own eyes counted for more.

Ignorance about elementary principles of statistical inference is another common culprit. The Israeli air force at one time noted that, when pilots were criticized after a bad performance, they usually did better the next time. When praised for a good performance, they tended not to do as well on the next occasion. The instructors concluded that criticism is effective in training pilots, presumably by forcing them to concentrate, whereas praise has the opposite effect, presumably by spoiling them. They were not aware of the simple statistical principle that a very good performance tends to be followed by a poorer one, while a bad performance is on the average followed by a better one. Baseball players who, after an outstandingly good season, do not do as well in the next are often unjustly criticized by trainers or fans as being spoiled by success. Also, people have difficulty understanding the notion of randomness. They tend, for instance, to underestimate the amount of clustering in a random process. Londoners during the blitz noticed that bombs fell in clusters and inferred, incorrectly, that there was an intentional pattern in the German bombing.

Finally, our lives can go badly for us because our desires are irrational. Since the very notion of rational and irrational desires is contested, I begin with an example that is relatively uncontroversial. If my desires focus heavily on the present, so that I engage in no long-term planning, I am likely to suffer in the long run.[15] This example suggests a definition of rational desires: they are desires such that given our opportunities, they make us as happy as possible. For a person with an iron constitution, a large fortune and a good lawyer, present-oriented desires could well be rational, but for those with fewer opportunities some concern for the future is needed. But on reflection, the

15 I am not referring here to weakness of will. As I said earlier, and will explain in the next chapter, there can be impulsiveness without weakness of will.

proposed definition is not adequate. Consider people who live in stable, totalitarian regimes. If there is an internal opposition of dissidents, they will tend to be unhappy. Their greatest desire is for political freedom, which is exactly what they cannot get.[16] Conversely, many people will be relatively content, because they entertain no desire for freedom and find all sorts of faults with societies that offer it. It would be absurd, I think, to say that the former are irrational and the latter rational. Although rulers of totalitarian regimes are wont to lock up dissidents in psychiatric hospitals, we should not accept their diagnosis.

We can amend the definition somewhat, by distinguishing between two mechanisms that have more or less the same outcome. On the one hand, there is the unconscious adaptation and adjustment to the opportunity set that is illustrated in the fable of the fox and the sour grapes. This takes the form, typically, not of upgrading what one can get, such as the sweetness of strawberries (or lemons), but of downgrading what one cannot get. When our minds play this kind of trick on us, it would be strange to say that the resulting desires are rational. They are, if anything, irrational. On the other hand, we can deliberately cultivate the good side of what we can have and try to reduce the intensity of our desire for what we cannot get. This is the method of rational character planning advocated in Buddhism, by the Stoics and by Spinoza.[17] On this construal of rational desires, we would not be compelled to say that supporters of totalitarian regimes are rational. We would still, however, have to say that dissidents are irrational, contrary to intuitive, preanalytical notions of what it is to be rational.

I do not know how to resolve this conundrum. Highly impulsive desires can plausibly be said to be irrational, because they are self-defeating. By yielding to spontaneity today, I reduce the

16 I am assuming here that their inability to get it is not the cause of their wanting it.
17 What Buddhism advocates is actually somewhat different. It tells one to reduce one's desires so as to be content with little, *even if one could have much* – because desires, even when fulfilled, produce more pain than pleasure.

number of occasions on which I can behave spontaneously in the future. Spontaneity is a value that must be protected by nonspontaneous concerns for the future. Also, there is an argument for saying that desires that come into being by disreputable causal mechanisms, operating behind the back of a person in a way that he would have been ashamed of had he been aware of it, are irrational.[18] These examples do not amount to a definition, but they do suggest that the place of reason could be more important than a literal reading of Hume's aphorism would indicate.

18 When I desire something simply because I cannot get it, the desire is both self-defeating and the product of a disreputable causal mechanism. The "sour grapes" mechanism is not self-defeating.

V

MYOPIA AND FORESIGHT

IN the state of nature – a fictitious state much discussed by
philosophers and somewhat reminiscent of the island in William Golding's *Lord of the Flies* – people live in the present and
care only about themselves. As a result, their lives, in Hobbes's
memorable phrase, are "solitary, poor, nasty, brutish, and
short." No known societies are quite like that. The Ik of Uganda,
as described by a social anthropologist who stayed with them
for some time, are probably as close to the state of nature as any
human group on record, but even they display minimal forms of
self-restraint.[1] A major task of the social sciences is to explain
why we are not in the state of nature.[2] Here I shall consider
foresight – the ability to be motivated by long-term consequences
of action – as a possible explanation of self-restraint. Other explanations are discussed later.[3]

I said in chapter III that rational choice is concerned with the
outcome of actions. It is often useful to think of an action as
generating an indefinite *stream* of (intended or expected) outcomes or consequences.[4] Suppose that after obtaining a college
degree in economics an individual has the choice between studying for a Ph.D. and taking a job in a bank. Each option has

1 I quote from his account in the next chapter.
2 This could mean two things. First, if we (or our animal ancestors) ever were
  in the state of nature, how did we get out of it? Second, what prevents us
  from sliding into it (or back into it)? The first question is briefly addressed in
  chapter VIII, but the main focus is on the second.
3 In the next chapter I look at altruism and similar nonselfish motivations and
  in chapter XII at the elusive phenomenon of social norms. In chapter XIII the
  various explanations are brought together in a more unified exposition.
4 Unintended consequences are the topic of chapter X.

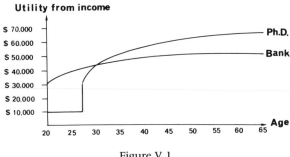

Figure V.1

associated with it a profile of earnings over time,[5] and each level of earnings has associated with it a certain level of utility or welfare (Fig. V.1).[6] We assume, for simplicity, that the individual is motivated solely by income, so that graduate study offers no intrinsic rewards that could offset, at least partially, the low income.

Under these circumstances, what will the individual choose? Clearly, it depends on how much importance he (presently) attaches to welfare at different times. If he is totally present-oriented, he will take the job in the bank. Studying for a Ph.D. is an indirect strategy, of the form "One step backward, two steps forward." It requires some ability to postpone gratification. At the other extreme, let us suppose that he attaches equal importance to all years in his life.[7] It might then appear as if he should opt for the Ph.D., since it gives him greater total welfare over the period from twenty to sixty-five. The snag is that he might not live to be sixty-five. Welfare in successive years must be discounted, therefore, by the probability of being dead. So if there

5 Assume, for simplicity, that after sixty-five there is no difference between the options. We also assume that it is not possible to borrow against future earnings.

6 Here we assume that utility functions remain constant over time. If young people get more (or less) welfare out of a dollar than old people, the argument would have to be restated correspondingly.

7 Actually, at the other extreme would be a person who thinks future welfare all-important and attaches no weight to welfare in the present.

43

is a 10 percent chance of being dead by sixty, the *present value* of welfare at sixty is only 90 percent of the welfare he will experience if he lives to be sixty. The correct procedure would then seem to be the following. For each option and for each year in the future, calculate the present value of the welfare I shall have under that option in that year. Next, for each option add up present values for all years in the future. Finally, choose the option with the largest present-value sum.[8]

Actual behavior is somewhere between these extremes. People discount the future more heavily than can be justified on the basis of mortality tables, although they certainly attach some weight to it. I believe this attitude is irrational. To discount the future simply because it is future is very much like irrational belief formation that attaches excessive importance to current events at the expense of past records. The future, like the past, isn't here, and that is why it counts for less than it should. Saving too little for one's old age is often a result of a failure of imagination. In other cases, the present overwhelms us by offering temptations that we cannot resist. When I take my second helping of cream cake, it is sometimes as if my rational self has lost charge. I can see that it is my hand which takes the cake, but it does so with no assistance from *me*. Other, more debilitating effects are drinking, cigarette smoking, drug addiction, adultery and gambling. In chapter XIII we shall see that noncooperative behavior can partly be accounted for by the same mechanism. A person who is not at all moved by the future consequences of his present behavior can

8 There is a problem that is being swept under the carpet here. Consider the interpersonal analogue to this personal decision problem. If a government is faced with two options, it may choose the one that maximizes total welfare. This is the analogue of the decision principle adopted in the text. But the government might also choose the option that maximizes the welfare of the worst-off group in society – protecting the weak rather than promoting the "greatest good for the greatest number." In the personal decision problem, the analogue would be to choose the option that has the highest minimum welfare associated with it, i.e., to take the job in the bank. (Note that here it would not be appropriate to discount for the likelihood of death.) This decision criterion is no less (and no more) rational than that of maximizing total discounted welfare.

confidently be expected to mess up his life – and that of other people.

Self-destructive behavior is not in itself a sign of weakness of will. A person who doesn't care about the future, or who cares consistently less about it than he does about the present, does not suffer the frustrating experience of doing what, all things considered, he would rather not do. That experience arises when the discounting of the future takes a special form, which prevents us from holding consistently to past decisions.

Suppose that, on January 1, I make an appointment with my dentist for January 21, not because I have a toothache but because I think it is a good idea to check my teeth regularly. I expect the dentist to find a cavity or two and to do some painful drilling, but I decide that the long-term health benefits will largely offset this acute but temporary suffering. On January 20, I call up the dentist to cancel the appointment, for no other reason than that it is now more imminent than when I made it. (I probably tell the dentist, though, that I have to go to a funeral.) What happened to make me change my mind?

Consider another example. My great uncle dies unexpectedly and leaves me a million dollars. I decide to use half of it on a big spree in the first year and then to live off the interest from the remaining $500,000. After the end of the first year, I change my mind. I now decide to spend $250,000 on a somewhat smaller spree in the second year and keep the rest in the bank for a rainy day. At the end of the second year, I change my mind again, and so on until little is left of the inheritance. Why was I unable to stick to my decisions?

These are examples of weakness of will. I decide to do something, but when the time comes to execute the decision I do something else. This phenomenon cannot be reduced to a tendency to favor the present over the future, or the near future over the distant future. That tendency might explain my never making an appointment with the dentist in the first place, but not my making it and then canceling it. It could explain why I spend most of my inheritance in the first year, but not why I

45

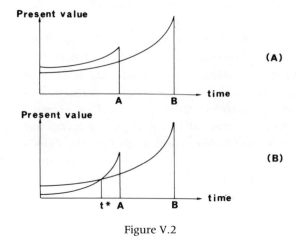

Figure V.2

form and then fail to carry out a plan to use the rest of it more prudently. The explanation of this inconsistent behavior is that the future does not decay – that is, lose its value, from the point of view of the present – at a constant rate as it moves away from the present. Rather, it first decays very rapidly and then more slowly. Figure V.2 makes it possible to state this more precisely.

In the diagrams, a person has the choice between an early, small reward A and a larger, delayed reward B. The choice has to be made at the time when A becomes available. The curves represent the present value of A and B at various times before their becoming available. The more distant the future time at which they become available, the lower is their present value.[9] The person's preferences at a given time are derived from a comparison of the present values of the options at that time: he prefers the one that has the largest present value. His inten-

9 In the diagrams, this is represented by the "present" moving to the left. Equivalently, it could be represented by the events A and B moving to the right. Statements about the rate of decay of the future should be read from right to left in the diagrams, so that a rapid initial decay of the future means that the curve first falls steeply and then more slowly as we move to the left.

tion at that time about what to choose later is based on that preference: he intends *now* to do *then* what he *now* prefers most.

In diagram A, the future decays at a constant rate:

$$\frac{\text{present value of a dollar today}}{\begin{array}{c}\text{present value of a dollar}\\\text{tomorrow}\end{array}} = \frac{\text{present value of a dollar tomorrow}}{\begin{array}{c}\text{present value of a dollar day}\\\text{after tomorrow}\end{array}}$$

In this case, the present has the same status relative to the near future as the near future to the more distant future. An implication is that, if one option is preferred to another at some time before the time of choice, it is preferred to the other at all times. In other words, the person will not change his mind as the time to consummate the choice approaches. Although he behaves impulsively, he is not subject to weakness of will.

In diagram B, the future first decays fast, and then more slowly:

$$\frac{\text{present value of a dollar today}}{\begin{array}{c}\text{present value of a dollar}\\\text{tomorrow}\end{array}} > \frac{\text{present value of a dollar tomorrow}}{\begin{array}{c}\text{present value of a dollar day}\\\text{after tomorrow}\end{array}}$$

Here the present counts for more relative to the near future than does the near future relative to the distant future. Because of this, *preference reversal* may occur. At time t^*, B ceases to be the most preferred option and A begins to look more attractive, right up to the time of choice. This is weakness of will – the inability to do what, all things considered, one believes one should do.

Studies of the behavior of animals – rats and pigeons – show that they discount the future in the way represented by diagram B.[10] There is evidence, although less conclusive, that human beings behave in the same way. To the extent that they do, they have a problem. Good intentions lose their power to motivate as

10 See chapter IX.

temptation approaches. The hope lies in learning from experience. Being irrational *and knowing it* is a big improvement over being naively and unthinkingly irrational. By coping rationally with my known propensity to behave irrationally, I may do better for myself than I can as the passive victim of that propensity. The techniques of coping are not costless, however, and sometimes the remedy is worse than the disease.

One way of coping is by acting on the opportunity set, as explained in chapter II.[11] When I make an appointment with the dentist, I can authorize him to bill me in full if I cancel.[12] If I inherit a million dollars, I can place half of it in a trust and make sure that I cannot touch the principal. Perhaps I want to save some money, but am frustrated by my tendency to spend my savings immediately. I can get around the problem by joining a Christmas saving club that will not allow me to withdraw my deposits until the end of the year.[13] If I want to quit smoking, I can announce my decision to the world so that backsliding is deterred by the fear of loss of prestige. To keep myself from drinking, I can take pills that will make me ill if I take a drink. If I am afraid that I may do something stupid at the Christmas office party, I can stay away. To prevent impulse buying in the supermarket, I can take with me just enough money to purchase the items on my shopping list. In some countries, a person can make a legally enforceable agreement with a drug clinic not to let him out within three weeks, even if he begs for it. If a government is afraid of yielding to popular pressures for deval-

11 To cope with weakness of will one can also act on one's desires, so as to make the temptation seem less attractive when it arrives. Weightwatchers religiously follow the principle "Never shop on an empty stomach." Some people ask to be hypnotized to acquire an aversion to smoking. This technique, while less costly than the others, is also much more rarely applicable.

12 Psychoanalysts, whose treatment may be even more painful than dentists', follow this practice but not, as far as I know, because their patients demand it.

13 Christmas club accounts usually pay lower interest than normal accounts, which shows that people are willing to pay for this substitute for self-control. One can also have it both ways, however, by depositing one's money in a high-interest account that has penalties for frequent withdrawals.

uation or wage increases, it can abdicate its responsibility to an independent federal reserve board or to the International Monetary Fund. Founding fathers may ensure that the constitution they create is hard to change, so as to prevent later generations from yielding to demagoguery.

These stratagems can be costly. Unforeseen events may make me wish I had not blocked out some opportunities. Ulysses might regret being bound to the mast if his ship comes into dangerous waters that his men cannot navigate on their own. The money I have saved but cannot touch may be needed for an important operation. Unless I am let out of the drug clinic for a few days my firm will go bankrupt. The federal reserve board may turn into a bastion of irresponsible monetary conservatism. The constitution can become the tyranny of the past over the present, saddling later generations with laws that have long outlived their usefulness. Ideally, Ulysses would want to be *loosely bound* to the mast – with ties strong enough to keep him from acting against his own better judgment, but not so strong as to prevent him from intervening in an emergency. Unfortunately, one can rarely have it both ways. One cannot anticipate all legitimate exceptions to self-binding contracts, and among the anticipated exceptions it is usually impossible for the enforcing party to distinguish between the genuine ones and those that were the raison d'être for the contract.

One can also cope with weakness of will by creating new principles for mental bookkeeping, without any intervention in the external world. The trick is to put oneself in a frame of mind in which one violation of the rule allows one to predict rule violations on all later occasions. "If I take a second helping of cream cake today, I'm just fooling myself if I think I won't do it the next time. Since there is nothing special about this occasion, the causes that make me yield to temptation today will have the same effect on the next occasion." By setting up this domino effect, I raise the stakes. One cigarette – just one – will inevitably lead me back to a pack a day. One drink, and I am on the slippery slope to ruining my life.[14] Although this stratagem of "bunching" the choices is a bit like magical thinking – as if I could change the cause by acting on the symptoms[15] – it can be very effective.

It can also be very costly, in terms of what it does to people's character and personality. Those who are deterred from impulsive behavior by the frightful specter of what would happen if they always acted impulsively tend to be rigid and compulsive. They do not get much enjoyment out of life, because they do not dare to give themselves a break, even when it would be manifestly harmless.[16] They are often referred to as Victorian character types – ridden by duty, hard on themselves and others. William James described their maxim as "Never suffer a single exception." Freud coined the term "superego" to describe the prohibitions and prescriptions that keep us in line when faced with temptation. In Freud's tripartite division of the mind, the ego – the autonomous self – is engaged in a two-front war against the totally myopic forces of the "id"[17] and the compulsive directives of the superego.[18] The autonomous individual seeks *loose bunching*, which allows him to indulge himself a bit without fear of unraveling a carefully constructed defense against his darker side.

The id is often said to belong to the *unconscious* part of the mind. I am not sure this is the right way to look at the matter. Recklessly impulsive behavior can be fully conscious. The core of truth in the view is that unconscious motivation is oriented

14 This effect should be distinguished from the bodily aspects of addiction. In the reformed alcoholic a single drink can have a purely physiological effect that will, in fact, trigger off an irresistible desire for more. The domino effect is all in the mind.

15 This is more fully explained in chapter XIII, which discusses an interpersonal instance of the same reasoning.

16 As mentioned in chapter IV, they may also, but in their very different way, suffer from weakness of will.

17 The Latin term for "it."

18 Freud believed that the superego is created in us by parental socialization. The argument in the text suggests that it can also be a purely individual construct.

toward the present and incapable of long-term, strategic calculation. For the the future to influence action in the present, it must somehow be anticipated in the present through the medium of consciousness. There is no evidence that we are capable of forming unconscious representations of the future. The unconscious cannot wait or use indirect strategies of the form "one step backward, two steps forward." Like water seeking the lowest level, it gravitates toward the actions that yield the greatest immediate pleasure, however dire the long-term consequences. Wishful thinking, for instance, yields powerful short-term gratification that can prove irresistible.

This argument has implications for psychotherapy. Suppose that a child whose parents quarrel frequently begins to act strangely. It is not unreasonable to think that the unhappy tension in the family has something to do with the child's problems. A therapist might explain the child's behavior as motivated by an unconscious desire to bring the parents together again. "If I get ill, they'll be worried about me and forget about their own problems." But if I am right, the therapist would have to be wrong. The unconscious could never behave in this strategic manner. The child's symptoms may well be caused by the unhappiness, but not by an unconscious desire to mend it.

VI

SELFISHNESS AND ALTRUISM

IN the state of nature, nobody cares about other people. Fortunately, we do not live in this dismal state. Sometimes we take account of other people's success and well-being and are willing to sacrifice some of our own for their sake.[1] Or so it appears. But perhaps altruistic behavior really springs from self-interest. For instance, isn't it in my long-term self-interest to help others, so that I can receive help in return when I need it? Isn't the patron of a charity motivated by his own prestige rather than by the needs of the beneficiaries? What matters to him is that his donations be visible and publicized, not who benefits from them.[2] Some might argue (see chapter II) that people are always and everywhere motivated by self-interest and that differences in behavior are due only to differences in their opportunities. Civilized society, on this view, depends on having *institutions* that make it in people's rational self-interest to speak the truth, keep their promises and help others – not on people's having good motivations.

I believe this argument is plain wrong, and I shall explain why in a moment. Let us first, however, get a few things out of the way. The proposition that self-interest is fundamental could

---

1 The second part of this sentence adds something to the first. I might take account of other people's interest only in the choice between two actions that serve my interest equally well.
2 Indeed, sometimes the motivating force seems to be the desire to give, and be known as giving, *more than other donors*. I was first struck by this motivation at the Art Institute in Chicago, where the size of the plaques honoring the donors is carefully adjusted to the size of the donation. What looks like altruistic behavior toward the public may in fact spring from emulation and envy of other donors.

be understood in two ways other than that just set out.[3] It could mean that all action is ultimately performed for the sake of the agent's pleasure or that self-interest has a certain methodological priority. The first view, again, is plain wrong. The second is true, but unhelpful as a guide to understanding behavior.

Consider first the view that all rational action must be self-interested because it is ultimately motivated by the pleasure it brings to the agent. An illustration could be love, often defined as taking pleasure in another person's pleasure. If I give a present to someone I love, am I not simply using that person as a means to my own satisfaction? Against this view, it is sufficient to point out that not all altruistic actions are done out of love. Some are done out of a sense of duty and need not provide any kind of pleasure. A person who is motivated by the warm glow that comes from having done one's duty is not acting out of duty, but engaging in narcissistic role playing. And in any case, the means–end theory of love is inadequate. I choose the gift to satisfy the other person's desire, and my own satisfaction is simply a byproduct.[4]

There is a sense, though, in which self-interest is more fundamental than altruism. The state of nature, although a thought experiment, is a logically coherent situation. But we cannot coherently imagine a world in which everyone had exclusively altruistic motivations. The goal of the altruist is to provide others with an occasion for selfish pleasures[5] – the pleasure of reading a book or drinking a bottle of wine one has received as a gift.[6] If

3 In addition there is the view, discussed in chapter VIII, that altruistic motivations can be explained in terms of "selfish genes."

4 Love is not the true converse of spite. A spiteful person acts to frustrate other people's desires because their frustration makes him feel good. Their suffering is instrumental to his welfare. The true converse of this attitude is the person who helps others because he likes to see happy faces around him.

5 This need not be true. A person may help his grandchild, to whom he feels indifferent, in order to give (nonselfish) pleasure to his child. But this presupposes that the child derives pleasure from the selfish pleasure of the grandchild.

6 When a small child buys a gift for his parents, they are often more touched by the act of giving than pleased by the gift – but they are touched only because they know the child was trying to please them rather than to touch them.

nobody had first-order, selfish pleasures, nobody could have higher-order, altruistic motives either. Some of the excesses of the Chinese cultural revolution illustrate the absurdity of universal altruism. All Chinese citizens were told to sacrifice their selfish interests for the interests of the people – as if the people were something over and above the totality of Chinese citizens.[7] The point is just a logical one. If some are to be altruistic, others must be selfish, at least some of the time, but everybody *could* be selfish all the time. The assumption that all behavior is selfish is the most parsimonious we can make, and scientists always like to explain much with little. But we cannot conclude, neither in general nor on any given occasion, that selfishness is the more widespread motivation.[8] Sometimes the world is messy, and the most parsimonious explanation is wrong.

The idea that self-interest makes the world go round is refuted by a few familiar facts. Some forms of helping behavior are not reciprocated and so cannot be explained by long-term self-interest. Parents have a selfish interest in helping their children, assuming that children will care for parents in their old age – but it is not in the selfish interest of children to provide such care.[9] And still many do. Some contributors to charities give anonymously and hence cannot be motivated by prestige.[10] Some forms of income redistribution are perhaps in the interest of the rich. If they don't give to the poor, the poor might kill them. But nobody was ever killed by a quadriplegic.[11] From a self-interested point of view, the cost of voting in a national election is much larger than the expected benefit. I might get a

7 The story by Garrison Keillor cited in chapter XIII could be used to illustrate the same point.
8 One might need only one selfish person, and all others could get all their pleasure from watching him and each other.
9 I am referring here to societies in which parents cannot disinherit their children.
10 Many, no doubt, would most like to have their cake and eat it too: to be well known as an anonymous donor.
11 And even when income redistribution is in the interest of the donors, it need not be motivated by that interest.

tax break of a few hundred dollars if my candidate wins, but that gain has to be multiplied by the very small probability that my vote will be decisive – much smaller than the chance that I will be killed in a car accident on my way to the polling place. And still a large number of people vote. Many people report their taxable income and tax-free deductions correctly, even when tax evasion would be almost riskless.

Some of these examples invite a counterargument. It *is* in children's rational self-interest to help their parents, because if they didn't their friends would criticize and perhaps desert them. It *is* selfishly rational to vote, because if one didn't one would be the target of informal social sanctions, ranging from raised eyebrows to social ostracism. I reply to these claims in chapter XII. Here I would simply like to make two points. It is not clear that it is in the rational self-interest of other people to impose these sanctions. And in any case the argument does not apply to behavior that cannot be observed by others. Anonymous contributions fall in this category, as does voting in many electoral systems.

Pure nonselfish behavior is represented by anonymous contributions to impersonal charities. Gifts to specific persons could be explained (although I don't really think so) by the donor's pleasure in giving pleasure. Publicly visible gifts could be explained by the prestige of donating or by the social sanctions imposed on nondonors. Only gifts from unknown to unknown are unambiguously nonselfish. On average, they amount to about 1 percent of people's income – not quite enough to make the world go around, but not negligible either if there are few recipients. When we add abstention from riskless tax evasion, the amount increases. Ambiguously nonselfish transfers are quite large. Since, in my opinion, the ambiguity can often be resolved in favor of the nonselfish interpretation, this makes the amount even bigger.

Let us look at the fine grain of altruistic motivation. Helping or giving out of love is instrumental behavior, that is, behavior concerned with outcomes. If I help my child, I seek the best means to make him happy. The concept of duty is more ambiguous: it can be instrumental or squarely noninstrumental. To begin with the latter, consider Kant's "categorical imperative," which, roughly speaking, corresponds to the question "But what if everyone did that?" What if everyone cheated on their taxes? What if everyone stayed home on voting day or refused to help the poor? This powerful appeal is not concerned with actual outcomes, with what would happen if *I* took a certain course of action. It is concerned with what would happen, hypothetically, if everyone took it. Suppose I am moved by the categorical imperative and try to decide how much I should contribute to charity. I decide on the total amount of charitable contributions that is needed, divide by the number of potential donors and donate the sum that comes out. If everyone did that, things would be just fine.

Now, in the real world, not everyone is going to do that. Many people give nothing. Knowing that, some would argue that it is their duty to give more than what would be needed if everyone did the same. They are motivated by actual outcomes of action under actual circumstances, not by outcomes under hypothetical circumstances. Because they are sensitive to outcomes and to circumstances, they give more the less others give. Conversely, if others give much, they reduce their contribution. To see why, recall the decreasing marginal utility of money (chapter III). If many have already given much, the recipients have a relatively high income, at which a further dollar adds less to their welfare than it does at lower levels. If one is concerned with the instrumental efficacy of giving, the motivation to give is reduced.

Kantians are concerned neither with outcomes nor with circumstances. The people discussed in the preceding paragraph — they are often called utilitarians — are concerned with both. People in a third category are concerned with circumstances, but not with outcomes. They look at what others are doing and follow the majority. If others give little, they follow suit; and similarly if others give much. The underlying motivation is a norm of *fairness*.[12] One should do one's share, but only if others are doing theirs. This motivation is insensitive to outcomes, as shown by the fact that it leads to exactly the opposite pattern of outcome-oriented utilitarianism. Suppose that we have had a big party, and next morning there is a great deal of cleaning up to be done. Everyone joins in, although the kitchen is small and we are tripping over each other's feet, so that the work is actually done less efficiently than it would be if some of us instead sat on the back porch. But the norm of fairness forbids free riding, even when everyone would benefit from it.[13]

Giving and helping are supposed to be in the interest of the recipients or beneficiaries. But how do we tell what is in their interest? The answer seems obvious: we find out by asking them. Sometimes, however, they cannot answer. Small children and mentally incompetent persons cannot tell us whether they want our help. We have to rely on some notion of objective interest, and usually that is not too difficult. Hard cases arise when people's expressed interest differs from what we, the donors, believe to be their real interest. The expressed interest might reflect an excessive preoccupation with the present, whereas we, the donors, want to improve their life as a whole. Such *paternalism* is relatively easy to justify when the relation is literally that of parent to child, but harder when the recipients are adults with full civic rights, including the right to vote. Giving food stamps instead of money is an example. If the recipients had voted for this mode of transfer, it would be an unobjectionable form of self-paternalism, as discussed in the preceding chapter, but that is not how these decisions are made. They are made by the welfare bureaucracy.

Paternalistic decisions should not be taken lightly. For one thing, the opportunity to choose – including the right to make the wrong choices – is a valuable, in fact indispensable, means

12 This norm, together with the categorical imperative and other social norms, is further discussed in chapters XII and XIII.
13 I am assuming, for simplicity, that we have no intrinsic pleasure just in being together.

to self-improvement. For another, there is a presumption that people are the best judges of their own interest. From the point of view of a middle-class welfare official, the values and priorities of the poor may seem crazy, but that is not really any of his business. His life style probably appears the same way to them. Paternalism is appropriate only when freedom to choose is likely to be severely self-destructive, especially when it will also harm other people.

Paternalism, even when misguided, is concerned with the well-being of the recipient. Gift giving can also, however, be a technique of domination and manipulation. It can serve the interests of the donor, against – and not through – the interests of the recipients. I can do no better here than to quote at some length from Colin Turnbull's account of gifts and sacrifices among the Ik:

> These are not expressions of the foolish belief that altruism is both possible and desirable: they are weapons, sharp and aggressive, which can be put to divers uses. But the purpose for which the gift is designed can be thwarted by the non-acceptance of it, and much Icien ingenuity goes into thwarting the would-be thwarter. The object, of course, is to build up a whole series of obligations so that in times of crisis you have a number of debts you can recall, and with luck one of them may be repaid. To this end, in the circumstances of Ik life, considerable sacrifice would be justified, to the very limits of the minimal survival level. But a sacrifice that can be rejected is useless, and so you have the odd phenomenon of these otherwise singularly self-interested people going out of their way to "help" each other. In point of fact they are helping themselves and their help may very well be resented in the extreme, but it is done in such a way that it cannot be refused, for it has already been given. Someone, quite unasked, may hoe another's field in his absence, or rebuild his stockade, or join in the building of a house that could easily be done by the man and his wife alone. At one time I have seen so many men thatching a roof that the whole roof was in serious danger of collapsing, and the protests of the owner were of no avail. The work done was a debt incurred. It was another good reason for being wary of one's neighbors. [One particular

individual] always made himself unpopular by accepting such help and by paying for it on the spot with food (which the cunning old fox knew they could not resist), which immediately negated the debt. (*The Mountain People,* New York: Simon & Schuster, 1972, p. 146)

Now, it would not be possible to manipulate the norm of reciprocity unless it had a grip on people, since otherwise there would be nothing to manipulate. Turnbull's account demonstrates both the fragility of altruism and its robustness.

Selfishness has a bad name, but compared with some other motivations it can seem positively benevolent. When people are motivated by envy, spite and jealousy, they have an incentive to reduce other people's welfare. The hard way of doing better than others is to improve one's own performance. The easy way is to trip up the competition. Taking pleasure in other people's misfortune is probably more common than actively promoting it,[14] but sometimes people do go out of their way to harm others at no direct gain to themselves. When a good – such as custody of a child – cannot be divided between the claimants, one response is "If I can't have it, nobody shall." A depressing fact about many peasant societies is that people who do better than others are often accused of witchcraft and thus pulled down to, or indeed below, the level of others. Against this background, ruthless selfishness can have a liberating effect.

Selfishness works best, however, when combined with a modicum of honesty. Honesty should not be confused with altruism. I keep my promise to you not because I care about your welfare, but because I care about my reputation as a person of honor. Cutthroat competition in the market may coexist with norms of honesty and promise keeping.[15] Unless constrained by

---

14 This poses a puzzle for rational-choice theory. Suppose I prefer state x, in which your desires are frustrated, to state y, in which they are satisfied. If offered an occasion to frustrate your desires, I should take it, even at some cost to myself. If I don't, am I irrational? Or am I coping rationally with an irrational desire, by refusing to act on it?

15 See chapter XII for a discussion of social norms.

social norms and minimal codes of honor, selfishness turns into opportunism. It is an ugly creature, no less unpleasant than envy in appearance and consequences. If traditional, envy-ridden societies are permeated by accusations of witchcraft, many transitional societies are subject to rampant opportunism, corruption and cynicism.

VII

EMOTIONS

EMOTIONS are the stuff of life. Anger, shame, fear, joy and love are immensely powerful states of mind. Subjectively, they are experienced as overpowering. We do not choose to have them; rather, we are in their grip. Our strongest emotions keep us awake at night, loosen our bowels, lend supernatural acuity or deep gloom to our perception of the world and help us achieve wonders when they do not leave us paralyzed. Other emotions are more subtle, less violent, yet no less central to our life. Hope and surprise, disappointment and regret, wistfulness and longing, envy and malice, pride and contentment: these are the hues of everyday life. An affectively neutral experience, if we can envisage it at all, would be pointless. Creatures without emotions would have no reason for living, nor, for that matter, for committing suicide.

The importance of emotions in human life is matched only by the neglect they have suffered at the hands of philosophers and social scientists. The nature, causes and consequences of the emotions are among the least well understood aspects of human behavior, matched only by our poor understanding of social norms (chapter XII), to which they are closely linked. There has been more speculation about than careful attention to these phenomena. Emotions have been explained in terms of their alleged benefits for biological survival, social cohesion or personal advance, not studied in their immediate vividness. Or attention is focused on the cognitive aspect of the emotions, once again at the expense of their raw motivational power. Often, emotions are seen mainly as sources of irrationality and as obstacles to a well-ordered life, disregarding the fact that a life without emotions would be wooden and, as I said, pointless. To understand the emotions, one must turn not to the social sciences but to world literature – or to oneself.

I shall have more to say about the relation between rationality and the emotions, but first a brief typology may be in order. Certain emotional experiences are inherently pleasurable and desirable. They arise from the enjoyment of beautiful sights, tastes and sounds; from love and friendship; from the use and development of one's powers and abilities; from the recognition of one's achievements by competent others. These emotions have a specific personal, temporal and modal structure. They derive from *my* experiences, not from those of other people. Moreover, they relate to my *current* experiences, not to my past or future ones. Finally, they derive from my *actual* experiences, not from those I may have or could have had. We may think of emotions with these qualities as *core emotions*. Although I have cited only the inherently positive core emotions, there are also inherently undesirable ones: disgust, fear, hate, shame, anguish. Anger also belongs to the core emotions, but is neither inherently pleasurable nor unpleasurable.

The other emotions are in various ways parasitic on the core emotions. They arise from the contemplation of earlier, future or possible occasions for the core emotions, from the loss or lack of such occasions or from the experiences of other people.

The emotions of anticipation and hope are directed toward the certain or possible future, as are those of dread and anxiety. Similar emotions are directed toward the past. Other things being equal, these backward- and forward-looking emotions have the same sign as the core emotions to which they make reference. A memory of a bad experience is a bad memory. Hope is a pleasurable experience because it is hope of a pleasurable experience, something we would rather have than not have. Sometimes, however, other things are not equal. One meal in the best French restaurant in the world may be a wonderful experience, to be cherished in memory for a long time.[1] But it may also have the effect of devaluing later meals in decent French restaurants, by setting a new standard for comparison. It is not clear, therefore, that I am always better off having a supremely good meal if I cannot afford more than one. Against Tennyson's "'Tis better to have loved and lost, than never to have loved at all," we may set John Donne's "'Tis less grief to be foul, than to have been fair."[2]

Consider next the "counterfactual" emotions, arising out of what could have happened but didn't. They include relief, regret, wistfulness and the like. They also include many of the aesthetic emotions, derived from the vicarious experience of reading a novel or watching a play. Given the infinity of things that could have happened, how do we single out some of them as the object of a counterfactual emotion? If the occasion turns upon a chance event, I am more disturbed by the possible worlds that branched off in the recent past than by those that could have begun only in the distant past. If it requires a very improbable coincidence,[3] I am less concerned than if I can tell a plausible story about how it might have happened. If the occasion could have come about by my intervention, my feelings of regret are more pungent than if there was nothing I could have done about it.

The feelings generated by the experiences of nonfictional others include spite, envy, pity and sympathy. The good or bad experiences of other people can make us feel good or bad. (By reflection, there is also the more complex feeling of enjoying other people's envy of oneself.) Again, these emotions can be decomposed into endowment effects and contrast effects. I may be affected simply by what others have or by the difference between what they have and what I have. As in the case of the

---

1 Compare Ibsen's "Only what is lost can be possessed forever."

2 Samuel Butler's parody of Tennyson adds a further dimension: "'Tis better to have loved and lost than never to have lost at all."

3 For instance, George Eliot's *Middlemarch* turns upon a massive coincidence that, to some extent, detracts from the pleasure of reading the book.

French meal we may ask about the net effect: does the pleasure
I derived from your enjoyment of life offset the pangs of envy I
suffer at your enjoying life more than I do?

An important element in many instances of other-oriented
emotions is the belief that "it could have been me." There is, in
other words, a counterfactual element in the emotions triggered
by other people's experiences. For the thought experiment to
have an emotional impact, one must not be too different from
the other person. Tocqueville noted that we do not feel envious
toward those far above us on the social scale, only toward our
immediate superiors.

The related feeling of being unfairly treated deserves special
mention. Sufficient conditions for the occurrence of this powerful emotion are the following. First, the situation is perceived as
morally wrong; second, it has been brought about intentionally,
not as the byproduct of natural causality or the invisible hand of
social causality; third, it can be rectified by social intervention.
Thus the feeling of injustice rests on the combination of "It
ought to be otherwise," "It is someone's fault that it is not
otherwise" and "It could be made to be otherwise," in addition
to the general counterfactual condition "It could have been otherwise." When one of the conditions is lacking, envy or resent-
ment may arise instead.

A further class of emotions is generated by loss rather than
lack, with grief and disappointment being felt if the core emotion is positive and relief if it is negative.[4] The cessation of an
emotional state – be it positive or negative – does not simply
bring us back to the earlier emotional plateau. Rather, it tends to
generate another emotional state of opposite sign. Consider a
person who has just discovered a lump in her breast and is

4 Language is not always adequate to describe our emotions. Although we have
different feelings when a disaster just misses us, when a probable disaster fails
to materialize and when an unpleasant state of affairs ceases to obtain, the
single word "relief" covers them all. By contrast, the corresponding emotions
defined with respect to positive core emotions are verbally distinguished as
regret, disappointment and grief.

extremely anxious. Upon hearing from her doctor that there is no possibility of cancer, her mood for a while turns euphoric before she returns to an affectively neutral state. Conversely, the interruption of a good sexual experience can create acute frustration before, once again, the person returns to a neutral state.

The repeated occurrence of such events can intensify the contrast effect. Drug addiction, for instance, is characterized by decreasing benefits[5] from actual consumption and increasing severity of withdrawal symptoms. People who have been married for a long time may not feel very strongly about each other any more, yet one spouse will feel deep and prolonged grief if the other dies. Conversely, parachute jumpers report that over time the before-jump anxiety diminishes (although it never disappears entirely), whereas the euphoric aftereffects increase in intensity. A similar pattern obtains if we compare the pleasures of consumption and the pleasures of self-realization. In Fig. VII.1 the pleasures and pains required from single episodes of consumption and self-realization are shown as depending on time within episodes and across episodes.

The consumption pattern is most strikingly illustrated in addictive behavior, but with some variations it is found quite generally. Certainly, the positive pleasures of consuming a given type of good fade over time. The pattern of self-realization is found in building a boat, writing an article or reading a book. The beginning carpenter finds his work boring and difficult, and even for the accomplished craftsman the initial act of concentration takes an effort. For many scholars, writing their first article was intensely unpleasant, mitigated only by the relief they felt when it was accepted for publication. Later, they may come to feel that without their work life would not be worth living,[6] yet

5 Compared with the preaddictive baseline.
6 Sometimes, however, the trend is in the opposite direction. Some scholars become less satisfied with their work as they grow more accomplished. As they learn more about their subject matter, they also learn more about the extent of their ignorance. When the circle of light expands, so does the sur-

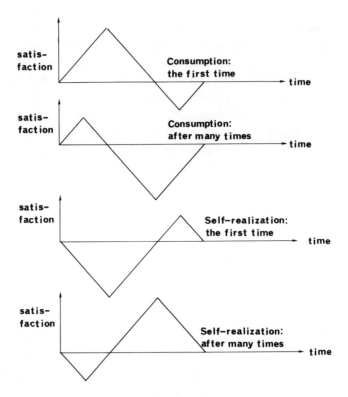

Figure VII.1

the initial stage of any piece of writing may still be so painful that they have to precommit themselves (chapter V) by writing against a deadline. Most novels are hard to get into, until one gets into the habit of reading novels. And the first pages of *Madame Bovary* are probably hard even for veteran readers.

In the short run, our emotional patterns are given. In the long

rounding area of darkness. Referring to nature, Emily Dickinson writes (*The Complete Poems of Emily Dickinson,* no. 1400, London: Faber & Faber):

> To pity those that know her not
> Is helped by the regret
> That those who know her, know her less
> The nearer her they get.

run, they are at least partially under our control. To the extent that they are, we can inquire into the emotional patterns that make for a good life. And even if they are not, we might still want to know why some people enjoy life more than others. Is there, as it were, an optimal set of emotional dispositions that can be achieved by choice or luck? If there is, it cannot be independent of external circumstances. If my life by and large goes well, a Stoic ability to endure adversity not only is pointless but is undesirable. To see why, note that one cannot choose emotions à la carte or, more generally, that emotional dispositions do not vary independently of each other. To ask for the ability to love without being vulnerable to grief is to ask for the moon, as is the desire to enjoy the euphoria of hope without being disappointed if the hoped-for event fails to occur. To be sure, "it's all in the mind," but the mind is not like a switchboard with one switch for each emotion. Because there are *couplings* between the emotions, a Stoic attitude comes at the cost of a flatter emotional life all round.

The couplings occur within the set of core emotions, between core and noncore emotions and within the latter. Consider first couplings within the core. Positive and negative emotions in the core are clearly correlated with each other. The propensities to feel pride and shame or euphoria and depression tend to wax and wane together.[7] Similar relations can obtain between emotions outside the core – for example, between hope and dread or between envy and malice. This commonsensical idea, that you cannot have emotional highs without also exposing yourself to emotional lows, also fits the Buddhist notion of character planning. For the Buddhist, the goal is to be rid of all emotions, not just the unpleasant ones.

Consider next couplings between the core and the emotions outside it. You cannot feel hope at the thought of X if you don't feel joy at the reality of X, nor dread X if you never feel anguish in its presence. At least, this is usually the case. In nonstandard

---

7 This is very much a simplification. Not all depressives are manic-depressives. Many persons who are prone to feelings of shame rarely feel proud of anything.

cases, a person might hope for a certain event to occur, yet not be able to enjoy it when it happens. Even in these cases, however, the hope would be logically parasitic on the core emotion, since its goal would still be the occurrence of the latter. I can't hope for *X* if I *know* I won't enjoy it.

Certain forms of love illustrate the nonstandard case. As traditionally conceived, love can be strengthened only if requited, because the goal of the lover is to be loved in return. In Racine's *Andromaque* Hermione asks the rhetorical question "Je t'aimais inconstant, qu'aurais-je fait fidèle?"[8] Clearly, the implied answer is that her love would then have been even stronger. Modern writers often give the opposite answer. Julien Sorel's relation to Mathilde de la Mole in *Le rouge et le noir* or the narrator's relation to Albertine in *A la recherche du temps perdu* is like a seesaw; when one is high, the other is low; love requited is love extinguished.

Hate offers a similar paradox, beautifully captured in John Donne's "The Prohibition":

> Take heed of hating me
> Or too much triumph in the victory,
> Not that I shall be mine officer,
> And hate with hate again retaliate;
> But thou wilt lose the style of conqueror,
> If I, thy conquest, perish by thy hate.
> Then, lest my being nothing lessen thee,
> If thou hate me, take heed of hating me.

Visceral hate can become so central to a person's life that it would lose all meaning if the object of hate were destroyed. The fanatical anticommunist needs communists to feed his hate, without which he is nothing.[9] The choice of "épater la bourgeoisie" as a life style similarly implies a dependence on one's en-

---

8 "I loved while you were inconstant; what would I not have done had you been faithful?"

9 On one interpretation, current communism itself is largely reduced to anti-Westernism, without any positive content of its own.

emy, which the latter may perceive as more sincere flattery than any imitation could ever be.

A central cluster of emotions – pride, shame, envy – is related to the need to believe in one's own worth. When we attempt to take stock of ourselves, the first impulse is to look at others. The serenity of mind that allows us to determine whether we are happy without comparing ourselves with others is rare. If the comparison is unfavorable, we feel a pang of envy, a fleeting rage.

The first urge of envy is not "I want what he has," but "I want him not to have what he has, because it makes me feel that I am less." There are different kinds of envy. A weak form is "If I can't have it, nobody shall." A more malignant form involves the willingness to cut off one's nose to spite one's face; to accept less for oneself if others are thereby brought down to one's own level. Inhabitants of small towns everywhere will recognize the "Law of Jante," written down (in 1933) by one who got away:

1 Thou shalt not believe thou *art* something.
2 Thou shalt not believe thou art as good as *we*.
3 Thou shalt not believe thou art more wise than *we*.
4 Thou shalt not fancy thyself better than *we*.
5 Thou shalt not believe thou knowest more than *we*.
6 Thou shalt not believe thou art greater than *we*.
7 Thou shalt not believe *thou* amountest to anything.
8 Thou shalt not laugh at *us*.
9 Thou shalt not believe that anyone is concerned with *thee*.
10 Thou shalt not believe thou canst teach *us* anything.
   (A. Sandemose, *A Fugitive Crosses His Track*, New York: Knopf, 1936, pp. 77–8)

These intensely social emotions play a major role in the operation of social norms (chapter XII). When a violation of a norm would provoke envy, the fear of being envied keeps deviants in line, a fear that, in turn, slides imperceptibly into the emotions of shame and guilt that are the main supports of social norms more generally.

Emotions matter because they move and disturb us, and because, through their links with social norms, they stabilize social life. They also interfere with our thought processes, making them less rational than they would otherwise be. In particular, they induce unrealistic expectations about what we can do and achieve, and unrealistic beliefs about other people's opinions about ourselves. In itself, this effect is deplorable. It would be good if we could somehow insulate our passions from our reasoning powers; and to some extent we can. Some people are quite good at compartmentalizing their emotions. Often, however, they don't have very strong emotions in the first place. They may get what they want, but they do not want very much. Granting supreme importance to cognitive rationality is achieved at the cost of not having much they want to be rational *about*. Conversely, lack of realism about our abilities and about the proper means for achieving our ends may be the price most of us pay for caring about life, knowledge or other people. When we are under the sway of strong emotions, we easily indulge in wishful thinking, such as the belief that all good things go together and that there is no need to make hard choices. The belief that one can have the motivating power of emotions without their distorting power is itself an instance of the same fallacy. Emotions provide a meaning and sense of direction to life, but they also prevent us from going steadily in that direction.

VIII

NATURAL AND SOCIAL
SELECTION

TO explain why people's behavior is adapted to their circumstances, one might argue that people who don't adapt don't
survive. Selection of the best, rather than rational choice, is
what ensures a tight fit between behavior and the demands of
the environment. These two mechanisms differ in a number of
ways.

Rational choice is concerned with the intended outcomes of
action. Selection mechanisms operate through actual outcomes.[1]
In explanations of animal behavior, where intentions have at
best a minimal place, actual outcomes must bear most of the
explanatory burden. It is more controversial which mechanism is
the most important in the study of human action.

As explained in chapter III, rationality is no guarantee of
success. Faced with a set of symptoms, doctors are acting rationally when they use what they have learned in medical school
to diagnose and treat their patients. If a disease is a novel one,
they can be quite wrong. Their frustrated patients may well turn
to quacks, who choose their treatments more or less at random.
One of them may accidentally hit upon a treatment that works.
Eventually all patients will receive that treatment, either because the lucky quack takes over the market or because others
start imitating him. In either case, the success of the treatment
owes nothing to rationality, and everything to accident and
selection.

Selection, for its success, depends on the raw material it has to

---

1 As will be explained in the next chapter, actual outcomes can also maintain or
eliminate behavior through the mechanism of *reinforcement*.

Utility, adaptation,
fitness, etc.

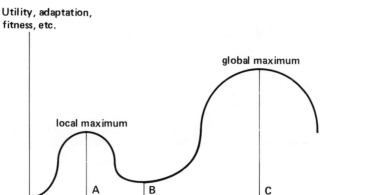

Some continuously variable determinant of utility, adaptation, fitness

Figure VIII.1

work on. If the right accident doesn't happen, or happens at the wrong time, the outcome may be far from optimal. Here rational choice is better placed. When I make a deliberate choice, I can survey a large number of alternatives, including many actions that have never been tried by anyone. I have a real chance of hitting upon the best alternative in the whole feasible set. Selection processes, by contrast, are restricted to the alternatives that are thrown up by chance. Often, these differ only in detail from the status quo. If an alternative is better than the status quo, it is selected; if not, it is rejected. Sooner or later the process will come to a halt, at a point where any further *small* change would be harmful, but that point may be far inferior to the best alternative in the feasible set, as illustrated in Fig. VIII.1.

Let us suppose we are dealing with some entity – an animal, a tool, a military unit or a firm – whose performance depends on some measurable feature of its structure or behavior. The performance itself is measured in utility, adaptation, fitness or whatever is relevant to survival. To fix our ideas for a moment, suppose that we are dealing with a flying object (an airplane or a bird), that the feature in question is the length of its wings and that performance is measured in speed. The relation between wing length and speed is supposed to be as in Fig. VIII.1. A rational plane constructor would choose wing length C, which yields the largest speed.[2] A selection process might not get that far, if it were constrained to move in small steps and to reject all changes that reduce the speed. If the wing length of a bird is initially to the left of A, any accidental reduction in wing length will be rejected. Any accidental increase will be selected as superior to the alternatives, as long as we remain to the left of A. Once A is reached, however, no further evolution by small steps can take place. To reach the global maximum at C, the selection process would have to pass through the minimum at B – but this is impossible since only changes for the better can be selected. Selection is stuck in a "local maximum trap," whereas rational choice can go straight for the global maximum.

The argument so far has been highly abstract and general, because it is intended to be valid for a number of selection mechanisms. It applies to the biological theory of natural selection, where it first arose, but also to the theory of economic competition, the theory of unconscious motivation and the theory of computer chess programs.[3] Before I consider the first two in more detail, I shall digress for a moment and say a few words about the relation between biology and the social sciences.

Generally speaking, scientific disciplines can stand in two sorts of relation to each other: reduction and analogy. Reduction takes the form of explaining phenomena at one level in the hierarchy of sciences in terms of lower-level phenomena (Fig. VIII.2). Reductionist research programs tend to be controversial.

---

2 To simplify, I neglect considerations of cost.

3 It follows from what was said at the end of chapter V that, because of its obeisance to the pleasure principle, the unconscious will always be stuck in a local maximum. The problem with computer chess programs (at least in the earliest versions) was that a good player could always exploit their greed or tendency to go for the quick gain, because there was an upper limit to the number of "steps backward" they could take.

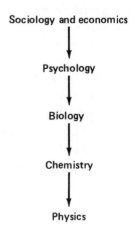

Figure VIII.2

For a long time, many vehemently claimed that the reduction of biology to chemistry could not possibly work – but it did. Many argue that sociology cannot possibly, or at least not today, be reduced to psychology. Since I insist that the individual human action is the basic unit of explanation in the social sciences, I am committed to this reduction.[4] A further step is the reduction of the social sciences – economics, sociology and psychology – to evolutionary biology. The discipline that tries to accomplish this reduction is called *sociobiology*. I shall have something to say later about the scope and limits of this discipline.

Reduction is at the heart of progress in science. Analogy is a much more dubious operation. In fact, the temptation to argue by analogy is perhaps the greatest obstacle to scientific progress. The social sciences, in particular, were late starters because they

4 I also believe, though, that in many cases it would be impracticable to try to carry it out. To understand the interaction among a large number of firms, one probably has to treat each firm as if it were an indivisible agent, although its decisions are really the outcome of complex internal processes.

looked to physics and biology for conceptual models, instead of searching for concepts appropriate to their subject matter. Biology, in particular, had a strong, durable and in the main disastrous influence. The analogy between organism and society suggested pseudoexplanations[5] and led to much waste of time in discussing pseudoproblems.[6] Less transparently absurd, and therefore all the more dangerous, was the inference that societies are inherently stable because, like any other organism, they have built-in mechanisms of defense and adjustment. Modeling economic competition as a mechanism similar to biological selection rests on a different analogy. Firms are seen as being analogous to organisms, struggling for survival in the competitive market. As we shall see, this analogy can also be seriously misleading.

The biological theory of evolution by natural selection rests on two mechanisms. First, it requires a mechanism to generate variety – raw material for selection. Ultimately,[7] all variety is generated by a steady stream of random changes, or *mutations,* in the genes – random in the sense in which typographical errors are random.[8] Like most typos, most mutations are harmful. Next, it requires a mechanism to select and retain the few mutations that happen to be useful.[9] Natural selection retains a mutation if the organism in which it has occurred can be expected to leave more offspring than others of the same species and in the

5 For instance, by comparing revolutions to fever or hysteria or by claiming that "it is no accident that" telegraph lines run parallel to railways just as nerves run parallel to arteries.

6 For instance, the debate whether the individual or the family is the social analogue of the cell.

7 In the short run, variety is also generated by the mixing of genes from each of the two parents.

8 The illustration is actually quite precise, since most mutations are errors in the process of copying genetic material.

9 Suppose a book contains some outdated statistics and that a typesetting mistake accidentally brings them up to date. (Here the analogy stops, since there is no mechanism by which the fortunate accident would increase the sales of the book.)

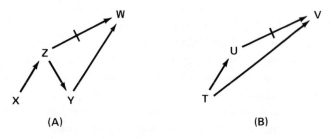

Figure VIII.3

same population.[10] Since the mutation occurs in the genes, it is passed on to the offspring. A mutation that favors more offspring will therefore be found in a larger proportion of the next generation of organisms. Eventually, it will be found in all organisms.[11] Further mutations may further increase the reproductive ability of the organisms, until a local maximum has been reached. It may, however, not be a global maximum, for reasons illustrated in diagrams A and B of Fig. VIII.3.

The figure illustrates the fact that, from a given genetic state, not all other states can be reached by a single mutation, since there are constraints on what counts as a coherent genetic instruction.[12] Unblocked arrows indicate feasible one-step moves, blocked arrows the unfeasible ones. Superior states are located

10 This sentence and the preceding one sweep a couple of important facts under the carpet. First, mutations can be neutral, that is, neither harmful nor useful. Neutral mutations create the possibility for random *genetic drift*. Second, even a useful mutation might not be retained, if its first bearer has the bad luck of being killed before it can reproduce. For these reasons, there is randomness not only in the production of mutations, but also in the process that determines whether they will be retained or rejected.

11 Unless the effect of the mutation depends on the number of organisms in which it is present. In that case, we might have the old and the new form stably coexisting with each other, in "frequency-dependent equilibrium" (see also chapter XI).

12 Consider the family game of going from one word to another, changing only one letter at a time and requiring all intermediate steps to be proper words. You can go from HAIR to HAIL in one step, but you need four steps to go from HAIR to DEAN. And I am fairly sure that no number of steps will take you from HAIR to LYNX, unless you go outside the dictionary.

above inferior ones. In diagram A, suppose the organisms are initially at X. They can reach the local maximum Z, but not the global maximum W. The direct path from X to W is blocked. The indirect path through Y is unfeasible, since any organisms in which that unfavorable mutation occurs will be wiped out. Organisms that take one step backward will not leave descendants that could take the further two steps forward. In diagram B, the organisms are initially at T, from where they can go either to the local maximum U, at which they will be stuck, or to the global maximum at V. If the mutation to U occurs first, the organisms cannot "wait" for the more favorable mutation to V. Natural selection operates in the present, unlike rational choice, which can be guided by the future.[13]

Natural selection improves the "fitness" – reproductive capacity[14] – of the individual organism. (An exception is discussed in the next paragraph.) It can very well have disastrous results for the population as a whole. Consider schooling in fish, that is, their tendency to swim in compact formations. Suppose that initially the fish swim in a more scattered way but that a mutation occurs that leads its bearer to seek the center of the group. This is a useful mutation, since that fish will receive greater protection from predators. As more and more fish behave in this way, the formation will become more and more compact, since every fish will try to be at the center. As a result, the predators' task will be made easier. More fish will get caught, as a result of a mutation that reduced the risk for each individual fish *compared with the prospects of others* that lacked the mutation.[15] What counts in natural selection is rela-

13 Note, however, that natural selection could program an organism to wait or to use indirect strategies in certain frequently occurring situations. A predator can be programmed to aim ahead of its prey, as if it anticipated the displacement of the moving target.

14 Note that fitness is not the same as adaptation to the environment. The latter, as measured, for instance, by expected life span, would be maximized by having no offspring at all, since the rearing of the young requires resources that the parents could have spent on themselves.

15 They are, in fact, in a Prisoner's Dilemma.

tive success – not absolute success. There is plenty of scope for spiteful behavior.

But there is also room for altruism – genetically based tendencies to sacrifice oneself. Birds, for instance, sometimes give warning cries that help others get away, even though the bird emitting the warning is running a risk by calling attention to itself. Such altruistic behavior is favored if the other birds are close relatives, bearers of the same gene for altruistic behavior. By sacrificing itself, the bird promotes the presence of the self-sacrificing gene in the population. Roughly speaking, it pays to sacrifice one's own life if one can save more than two brothers, four half-brothers or eight first cousins.[16]

The theory of natural selection has been very successful in explaining details of animal and human physiology, such as protective coloring or the puzzling persistence of genetically based anemia. There has been some success in explaining animal behavior, but little so far in accounting for human behavior. The main obstacle to sociobiology is that people don't behave in the rigid, stereotyped way that most animals do. They don't have hard-wired into their genes instructions for what to do on each occasion they are likely to encounter. Rather, what they do results from genetic predispositions interacting with the environment in ways that we do not understand very well. We don't know what limits, if any, "human nature" sets on the degree of peacefulness, altruism or monogamy that can be fostered by appropriate social institutions. Also, much sociobiological thought neglects a massively important feature of human beings: their creativity or general capacity for problem solving. Any particular human behavior must first be understood as an application of this ability to the problem at hand, along the lines discussed in chapter III. The evolutionary basis of that ability is only dimly understood, and in any case is not something social scientists

---

16 There is another evolutionary theory of altruism that aims at explaining altruism toward strangers, and even toward members of different species. This account is closely related to the theory of cooperation in repeated Prisoner's Dilemmas, further discussed in chapter XIII.

need to concern themselves with. Sociobiologists do not offer a rival explanation, but a supplementary one.

Although evolutionary biology offers an explanation of optimal behavior, it does not refer to any intention to optimize. This made it seem a good model for solving a problem that economists encounter in their study of the firm. On the one hand, firms appear to adjust and adapt optimally to their environments. On the other hand, close-up studies of firm behavior show little evidence that they are consciously trying to maximize profits. Rather, they use rough-and-ready rules of thumb – frozen accidents of history, or perhaps the outcome of internal bargaining processes. The two findings can be reconciled if economic competition is viewed as a selection process. A firm is characterized by a set of routines, just as an organism is by its genes. Firms that happen to use profit-maximizing routines do better than others. As a result, these routines spread in the population of firms, by takeovers or imitations.

We might try to explain technical change in this perspective. At one level, a firm's technique is a routine. At a higher level, firms have routines for innovating – for changing techniques. Suppose that initially a firm is doing quite well. Since it obeys the high-level routine "Never change a winning team," it has no incentive to change techniques. Suddenly, profits drop below a critical level, defined by the firm's aspiration level or concept of "winning." As a result, it decides to look for new and more efficient methods of production. Part of the search effort simply involves looking at what other firms are doing, and part involves genuinely innovative activity. After a while, a technique is found that yields profits above the critical level, and the search is switched off. Ultimately, all other firms adopt the new technique. The process differs from biological evolution, since the firm does not produce a steady stream of new techniques corresponding to the steady stream of mutations. Rather, the stream of "mutations" is switched on and off as needed.

The process could also lead to a change in high-level routines. The old routine "Never change a winning team" reflects the idea that necessity is the mother of invention. Don't innovate unless and until you have to. But as I mentioned in chapter II, this is a risky strategy, because when profits drop the firm may not have resources to innovate. Firms following this routine tend to go out of business, or at least to do badly on the average. Firms that survive and prosper follow another routine. They innovate when they are ahead and have the resources to do so, not when they are falling behind.

To see where this kind of argument goes wrong, we need to introduce a complication neglected so far. This is the fact that any selection process takes place in a changing environment. Since fitness is always fitness relative to the environment, an organism or a firm can grow unfit simply by virtue of standing still in a changing world.[17] There are, in other words, two processes going on at the same time. On the one hand, the environment is changing. On the other, units of selection – genes, organisms, routines or firms – are adapting to the environment.[18] Selection has a *moving target*. It is a brute fact of natural selection that the organic environment changes slowly relative to the process of adaptation. The adjustment, therefore, can be fine-tuned and close to the theoretical optimum. In economic competition, the environment changes very fast – much faster than the process whereby unsuccessful firms go bankrupt and successful firms expand. Rather than steady progress toward a state of optimal adaptation, economic selection would produce a zigzag course that at no point would be very close to what would be optimal at that time. The social-selection argument may work in slowly changing peasant societies in which there is time for tools and routines to reach local perfection. It is unlikely to have much explanatory power in complex, rapidly evolving economies.

17 An example was given in chapter IV: the firm should invest little in research and development if other firms invest much, and much if they invest little. There is no strategy that is best at all times.

18 The two processes are related, since the environment is partly made up of other evolving units. The example in the preceding note provides an illustration.

This argument, combined with that of chapter IV, suggests that optimal adaptation will be an exception rather than the rule. In general, neither subjective nor objective mechanisms can be trusted to make people do what it is in their interest to do. Rational choice is often indeterminate and cannot be counted on to yield optimal behavior, even assuming that people get rid of their tendencies to behave irrationally. Selection processes work too slowly to produce behavior that is optimally adapted to a rapidly changing environment. The next chapter suggests that the mechanism of reinforcement is no more likely to force optimal behavior.

IX

REINFORCEMENT

A T the end of chapter II, I mentioned how a child might develop nervous symptoms as a result of her parents' quarreling. I also discussed the implausible idea that she might unconsciously have adopted these symptoms *in order to* make her parents stop quarreling. But there is another possibility. Suppose that the parents do indeed stop quarreling when they see that they are making the child unhappy. From the child's perspective, she is *rewarded* for her symptoms. Although the symptoms arose independently of any intended effect on the behavior of the parents, their actual effect tends to *reinforce* them. The *function* of the symptoms, on this account, is to keep the parents from quarreling.[1]

This particular example of reinforcement may or may not be a plausible one, but there are plenty of cases in which this mechanism is the best explanation of behavior. We meet people more or less at random and cultivate as friends those whose company we like. We try out cooking recipes more or less at random and retain those that happen to please our spouse. Often, we do not do things for pleasure, but because they give us pleasure. In these cases a certain form of behavior has valuable or pleasurable consequences, and our perception or registration of that fact strengthens or reinforces our tendency to engage in it.

The consequences need not be the conscious goal of action. In fact, to distinguish reinforcement from rational choice it is useful to define it by stipulating that the reinforcing consequences not

---

1 This general theme – that unintended consequences of behavior can maintain that behavior – is discussed in the next chapter.

be deliberately sought. If a boy's temper tantrums are reinforced by the attention they get him, it would usually be false to say that getting attention is the goal of his behavior. Subjectively, he is more likely to experience the situation as one in which he does *not* get what he wants and, therefore, is angry.[2] A painter may be encouraged by the appreciation of his peers, but it would usually be false to say that the desire for appreciation is what motivates him when he paints. What motivates him is the desire for "getting it right," although the appreciation of others may enter into an explanation of the strength of that motivation.[3]

The reinforcing event – it may be a reward or a punishment – is more likely to shape behavior the sooner it occurs, the more certainly it occurs and the more frequently it occurs. The satisfaction of thirst by drinking is immediate, certain and frequent, and hence capable of shaping behavior in the most direct way imaginable. Getting cancer of the pancreas from drinking coffee is a consequence that is very unlikely to reinforce behavior. If one gets cancer from coffee, there is a delay of several decades; only a few get it; and they live only once. As a less extreme example, consider the risk of getting pregnant. Only in the past fifty years or so has it been known that the greatest chance of becoming pregnant is during the time between two menstruations. If every intercourse led to pregnancy, this insight could have emerged earlier. Similarly, it might have emerged earlier if the first signs of pregnancy occurred within one hour of conception or if every woman became pregnant hundreds or thousands of times in her lifetime.

Most social situations are of this kind. They have too little regularity, and too much noise, for reinforcement to shape behavior in a fine-tuned way. The major exception is the emotional gratification or deprivation that people who live closely together can offer each other. Parents shape children's behavior

2 If he threw a tantrum for the purpose of getting attention, he would probably not get it.

3 Painters who think more about the appreciation of others than about getting it right will rarely get it right and not be much appreciated either.

by showing their pleasure or displeasure. Spouses reward and punish each other in innumerable ways that shape their relation to each other. In stable, unhappy marriages each spouse is rewarded by the momentary glee that comes from provoking the other into displaying her or his worst behavior. In stable, happy marriages, the reward of each is the reward of the other. But if we want to explain voting behavior in Congress, the hiring policies of firms or patterns of geographical mobility, reinforcement is not a plausible mechanism. Intended consequences may count for much, but actual consequences are not sufficiently regular to feed back on behavior.

Exactly how consequences can reinforce motivation without being part of it is somewhat mysterious, but the fact is that they can. Animal behavior is not animated by conscious intentions,[4] but it is certainly guided by consequences. In fact, almost all that is *known* about reinforcement comes from the study of animal learning and adaptation – the rest is mainly extrapolation and speculation.

In studies of reinforcement, the animal – usually a rat or a pigeon – is given a choice between two activities, which are rewarded differently. A real-life analogy is the search for food in each of several environments. The task is to explain how much the animal engages in the one or the other. Typically, each activity (or *response*) takes the form of pecking a key or pressing a lever. There are two basic ways of attaching rewards to responses. On the one hand, we can set up a constant probability of reward for each response. The one-armed bandit of the Las Vegas variety illustrates this reward mechanism. It is a mechanism that has no memory: if we hit the jackpot on one occasion, the chances of hitting it again on the next occasion are not

---

4 This is somewhat controversial. Strong evidence of intentional behavior in animals would be provided if they could be shown to use indirect strategies in novel situations for which they could not have been programmed by natural selection. Some evidence of this kind of behavior exists for the higher primates, but not to my knowledge for the rats and pigeons that have been most extensively studied by reinforcement theorists.

modified. On the other hand, we can set up a mechanism with memory, so that each unrewarded response increases the probability that the next response will be rewarded. In practical terms, this could work as follows. In each period the experimenter uses a chance device, with constant probabilities, to decide whether to make food available. Once it has been made available it stays available. After the first period, let us assume, there is a 20 percent chance that the food is available; after the second a 36 percent chance; after the third, a 49 percent chance, and so on.[5] The animal does not know, however, whether it is available. To find out and to get the food, it must make the appropriate response (press the lever or peck the key). It can make two sorts of errors: respond before the food is made available and not respond when it is available.

The central question in reinforcement theory is whether animals allocate their responses optimally between the two activities, that is, whether they act so as to maximize their rewards. It turns out that the answer depends on the reward mechanisms associated with the two activities. If both reward mechanisms are of the one-armed-bandit type, animals often do the rational thing and allocate all their attention to the activity with the highest probability of reward. Sometimes, however, they commit the "gambler's fallacy" of distributing the stakes in proportion to the odds. If both mechanisms are of the other kind, findings are also ambiguous. With one mechanism of each kind, as in Fig. IX.1, animals usually do not optimize.

The animal can allocate between 0 and 100 percent of its time to the two activities. One is rewarded by a VR (variable-ratio) mechanism: this is the one-armed bandit. The other is rewarded by a VI (variable-interval) mechanism: this is the mechanism

5 To see how this calculation works, consider the probability that food will *not* be available at the end of the second period. This requires two chance events, each of probability 80%: that food will not be made available in the first period and that it will not be made available in the second. The probability that both of these will occur is the product of their probabilities, or 64%. Therefore, the probability that food *will* be available is 100 − 64 = 36%.

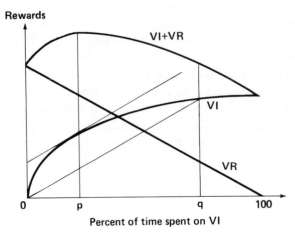

Figure IX.1

with memory. The VI curve shows total reward from the VI activity as a function of the proportion of time allocated to it. Its shape reflects the fact that the expected reward from each extra response decreases with the number of responses. If the animal responds on VI very rarely, the chances of being rewarded are very high on each occasion, since a long time will have passed since the last visit. If it responds very frequently, the chances are smaller. The VR curve should be read from right to left. When the animal allocates 100 percent to VI, it allocates nothing to VR. As less and less is spent on VI, more and more is spent on VR. The expected reward for this activity is simply proportional to the number of VR responses, since any response has the same chance of hitting the jackpot and being rewarded.

A rational animal should spend most of its time working steadily on the VR activity and occasionally visit the VI alternative to collect any reward that might have come due after its last visit to it. This intuitively plausible idea can be stated more precisely with the help of Fig. IX.1 Clearly, the animal's interest is to choose a proportion that will maximize the sum of the VI and the VR rewards. This occurs when it spends p percent of its time on VI and the rest on VR. An alternative way of expressing the same idea is that the animal should choose a VI–VR mix in which both activities have the same marginal value.[6] Suppose, for concreteness, that the animal responds 1,000 times to VI and 2,000 times to VR. The marginal value of VI – that is, the value of an extra response to VI – is the difference between the reward to 1,001 responses and the reward to 1,000 responses. Against this gain, we must set the loss of responding 1,999 instead of 2,000 times to VR. If the gain exceeds the loss, the animal is not optimizing: it could do better by changing its response mix. Conversely, an optimizing animal uses a response mix that cannot be improved upon.

It turns out, however, that animals don't behave optimally. Instead of spending the optimal p percent on VI, they spend q percent. Instead of equalizing the marginal values of the two activities, they equalize the average values.[7] The average value of VR is constant and equal to its marginal value. The average value of a particular level of VI is given by the slope of the line from that point on the VI curve to the origin. With the activity mix corresponding to q, the average value of VI equals that of VR. When animals equalize average values, they forget, as it were, that most of the VI rewards come from a few responses and that it isn't really profitable to go on paying attention to this activity. They don't see that the reward to each piece of VI activity depends on the total amount of this activity they are engaging in.

It is not clear whether this deviation from optimality is found in human behavior. Controlled experiments with human subjects are difficult. Also, the human capacity for conscious choice and the complexity of human affairs tend to reduce the importance of purely mechanical reinforcement. Yet to the extent that human behavior is shaped by reinforcement, as suggested by some earlier examples, similar effects may be expected.

6 In the diagram, VR has constant marginal value. The marginal value of VI is shown at point p and corresponds to the slope of the tangent to the VI curve at that point. When the animal optimizes, the slope equals that of the VR line.
7 This principle is called the "matching law."

Reinforcement experiments also yield important information about time discounting. Suppose that if a pigeon pecks a red key it gets immediate access to food for 2 seconds. If it abstains from pecking, it has access for 4 seconds, but with a delay of 3 seconds. Pigeons are greedy and invariably prefer the earlier, smaller reward. Suppose, however, that the key lights up green 12 seconds before it is due to light up red. By pecking the green key the pigeon can prevent it from lighting up red, thus eliminating the opportunity to be greedy. Some pigeons take this option. They evaluate the future as in diagram B in Fig. V.2,[8] and precommit themselves to get rid of temptation.

8 In fact, this evaluation can be derived from the matching law.

Part Three

INTERACTION

X

UNINTENDED CONSEQUENCES

THINGS don't always turn out as we expect them to. Many events occur unintentionally. In Adam Ferguson's memorable phrase, "History is the result of human action, not of human design." His contemporary, Adam Smith, referred to an "invisible hand" that shapes human affairs. Half a century later, Hegel invoked the "cunning of Reason," and thirty years after him Marx talked about people's "alienation" from their own action. The theme of unintended consequences of action was one of two central concerns of the emerging social sciences in this period, the other being the vision of society as an organic unity. These two images are still with us. On the one hand, there is the idea of individual actions interfering with each other to produce an unintended outcome. On the other hand, there is the idea – more fully discussed in the next chapter – of mutual adjustment among individual plans, allowing all to be carried out without distortion.

Before I consider the unintended consequences that arise from social interaction and interference, I would like to point out some mechanisms that operate within the mind. As explained earlier, an action is the result of desires and opportunities. But action can also shape desires and opportunities, in unintended ways (Fig. X.1).

In addition to the intended outcome of an action, there is sometimes an unintended one: a change of desire. Addiction is a simple example. What I desire may be another drink, but what I get may be the drink *and* a stronger desire. If I had known, I might not have taken the drink. Desires can also be affected in the opposite way, by a drive for novelty. In H. C. Andersen's

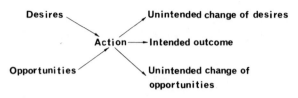

Figure X.1

story "What Father Does Is Always Right," a farmer goes to the market in the morning to sell or exchange his horse. First, he meets a man with a cow, which he likes so much that he exchanges it for the horse. In successive transactions, the cow is then exchanged for a sheep, the sheep for a goose, the goose for a hen and, finally, the hen for a sack of rotten apples. The farmer's road to ruin is paved with stepwise improvements.[1] Each time the farmer believes himself to be better off by the exchange, but the net result of all exchanges is disastrous.[2] What goes wrong is that, along with each new object, he acquires an unexpected new taste. If he had been able to anticipate the slippery slope, he might not have started on it. Although the story doesn't say so, it is likely that the farmer would have refused to exchange his horse for a sack of rotten apples. Curiosity and the thirst for novelty are triggered by options that are neither too similar to nor too dissimilar from the current state.

Actions can also have an unintended impact on opportunities. I know that drinking affects my purse, but that is one of the

---

1 Actually he is not ruined, because a pair of English tourists make and lose a bet that his wife will be angry with him when he comes back with the apples.
2 More formally, imagine a person who regularly (although not consciously) adjusts his desires so that he prefers more strongly the commodity of which he currently has less. Suppose he is exposed to the following sequence of two-commodity bundles: $(\frac{1}{2}, \frac{3}{2})$, $(\frac{3}{4}, \frac{1}{2})$, $(\frac{1}{4}, \frac{3}{4})$, $(\frac{3}{8}, \frac{1}{4})$ .... Then, if at a given time he is consuming bundle n in the sequence and for the next period is offered the choice between bundle n and bundle $n + 1$, he will always choose the latter, which offers more of the commodity of which he has currently less. But since the sequence converges to zero, these stepwise improvements pave the road to ruin.

expected consequences that are part of my decision. I may not know, however, that it also affects my health and thus my future ability to derive pleasure from other activities. At any given time, drinking may seem like a good idea, but if I take all occasions to drink I may end up in very bad shape. The interference among one person's choices at different points in time is a bit like the interference among the choices of different persons. If I always do what seems best at the moment, I may end up worse at all times.[3] If each person does what is rational, all may lose.

Turning now to unintended consequences that arise because of interaction among several persons, let me begin with a famous example from economic theory, the "cobweb," also called the "hog cycle" because it was first put forward as an explanation of cyclical fluctuations in hog production. It has a much wider application, however. Fluctuations in the shipbuilding industry in recent decades had very much the same pattern, with a seller's market followed by overinvestment and glut.

Hog farmers must decide one year ahead of time how much they want to market in the next year, a decision that is determined by the price they expect hogs to fetch and by the cost of producing them. An increase in expected price will induce farmers to produce more, as reflected in the upward-sloping supply curve in Fig. X.2.[4] The actual price at which hogs are sold will

---

3 This cannot be literally true, since at the time of the first drink I can enjoy both the drink and good health. At a given moment in time a person can suffer harm only from what he has done at earlier moments; what he may do later cannot yet hurt him. But one person may be hurt by what all others do.

4 This supply curve is really the sum of many individual supply curves, one for each farmer. Each point on an individual supply curve shows the profit-maximizing volume at the given price. At that volume, the marginal cost (the cost of producing one more hog) equals the price of a hog. When the price goes up, production expands to the point where the marginal cost is once again equal to the price. Marginal cost rises because each farm operates with given equipment which becomes a bottleneck when production expands. Although some parts of the equipment (buildings, etc.) can be easily expanded without loss of efficiency, others (notably decision-making capacity) cannot.

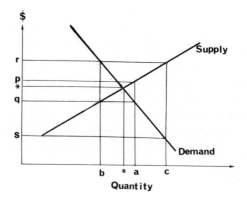

Figure X.2

determine how much consumers buy, as reflected in the downward curve.[5] If producers, expecting one price, market more than consumers will buy at that price, competition among producers will force the price down until the market clears. If they market less than consumers will buy, competition among consumers will force the price up until the market clears. Equilibrium – marked by asterisks in the figure – occurs when expected price equals realized price, and producers sell all they produce at the price that induced them to produce it in the first place.

The simplest way of forming a price expectation is to assume that next year's price will be like this year's price. In Fig. X.2, suppose that the price in year 1 is *p*. Expecting this price to prevail in year 2 as well, producers offer volume *a* in year 2. Consumers, however, are not willing to buy this quantity at that price, and the price is forced down to *q*. Acting on the assumption that the price will remain constant from year 2 to year 3, producers offer volume *b* in year 3. As a result, the realized price *r* exceeds the expected price. Expecting *r* to prevail in year 4, producers offer volume *c*, but to sell it they have to accept the

5 This curve, similarly, is the sum of many individual demand curves for hogs. They slope downward because consumers turn to other products as hogs become more expensive.

all-low price *s*. The movement of prices and volumes forms a sort of cobweb, spiraling outward from the equilibrium.[6] Prices and incomes are alternately higher and lower than the expected ones. Pleasant surprises alternate with unpleasant ones. The expected outcome never occurs.

Voting behavior can illustrate the same mechanism. Polls published before voting day can influence actual voting, in several ways. Some voters want to get on the bandwagon and switch their vote to the candidate with the higest standing in the polls. Others favor the underdog, perhaps because they believe it important that the loser not lose too much. The underdog reasoning could, however, be self-defeating if sufficiently many acted on it. For each voter, the reasoning makes sense only if all or most other voters conform to the poll's predictions – that is, if they do not behave like him. But if many people switch to the underdog on the assumption that few will switch, they are in trouble. Collectively, they could end up voting the candidate into office when, individually, they wanted only to assure him of a decent standing.[7]

The most striking unintended consequences make everybody worse off. Jean-Paul Sartre referred to this as "counterfinality," using erosion as an example. When farmers try to get more land by felling trees, they can end up losing land because large-scale deforestation leads to erosion. Instances of counterfinality abound. When everyone gets to his feet to get a better view of the game, no one succeeds and all get tired from standing up. When all are motivated by the desire to earn a bit more than their neighbors, they end up running as fast as they can in order to remain in the same place. When all heads of families decide to have many children who can take care of them in their old age, the ensuing overpopulation can make everybody worse off. When everybody simultaneously tries to take money out of the

6 With different slopes of the supply and demand curves, the movement would have been an inward spiral converging to the equilibrium.
7 It could happen, however, that the underdog effect is offset by the bandwagon effect, so that actual results correspond to the predicted results.

bank, all may lose their deposits. When all firms try to weather a recession by cutting wages, the ensuing loss of purchasing power can turn the recession into a full-fledged depression.

Let us consider the last example in more detail. Firms stand in a twofold relationship to workers. Since they need workers as customers for their products, they have an interest in high wages so that workers can spend more. But since firms also employ workers, they have an interest in low wages. Ideally, the individual firm would want its workers to receive low wages and the workers employed by all other firms to receive high wages. There is no logical obstacle to a firm having it both ways, although in a competitive labor market it would not happen. What *is* logically impossible would be for all firms to have it both ways – for each and every firm to be the only one to pay its workers low wages.[8]

But unintended consequences can also make everybody better off. This is Adam Smith's invisible hand: the pursuit of self-interest serves the common interest. A firm that introduces new technology is motivated exclusively by its own profits, yet by making consumer products (or inputs used by other firms) less expensive, it indirectly serves the common interest. Consumption for private benefit creates employment – and thus consumption opportunities – for other people.[9] People paint their houses to protect them from bad weather, but in doing so they may also offer others the benefit of a pleasant sight. If all members of a community keep an eye on their own children while they are out playing, they cannot help also watching each other's offspring. As a result, everybody's children are given greater protection.

8 The belief that what could be true for *any* unit taken separately could also be ture for *all* units taken simultaneously is sometimes called the "fallacy of composition." We commit it when we apply the marginal tax rate to calculate the real cost of all tax-deductible items, thus forgetting that only one dollar can be the last dollar.
9 This was a cherished idea of Adam Smith's forerunner, Bernard Mandeville, whose slogan "Private Vices, Public Benefits" is perhaps the earliest statement of the invisible-hand mechanism.

Counterfinality and the invisible hand have a common structure. A person acts in order to benefit. In doing so, he also affects other people (and often himself)[10] in a secondary way. Typically, the secondary impact, whether negative or positive, is quite small compared with the primary, intended benefit. Yet when everybody acts in this way, each person becomes the target of many small benefits or many small harms. (These small side effects are usually referred to as *externalities*.) If the secondary effect is positive, we have an invisible-hand mechanism. If it is negative, there are two possibilities. Either the sum total of the many small harms exceeds the primary benefit (this is counterfinality), or the primary benefit exceeds the cumulative harm. Everybody is made better off by acting in the specified way, but less well off than they expected to be. Some examples of counterfinality suggested earlier could, in modified form, also illustrate this case.[11]

In these illustrations, the persons whose actions have unintended consequences are also those who suffer or benefit from them. Equally important and numerous are cases in which the consequences are felt by other people. In traditional China, many poor families practiced infanticide of girls. The result was a surplus of boys, and a substantial number of unmarried young men who were excellent material for recruitment by bandits. The victims of banditry were mainly landlords and well-to-do peasants, who did not practice girl infanticide to the same extent. Predation on the rich was an unintended consequence of

10 A firm is somewhat hurt by cutting the wages of its own workers, since they spend some of their income, if typically a very small part, on the firm's products. Or consider a computer firm that comes up with a new design. The primary benefit for the firm is that it makes a profit by selling the new computer. A secondary benefit is that it can use the computer in its own operations.

11 Assume that, before deforestation, the peasants had ten thousand acres of land, half of it cultivable and half of it wood. After deforestation, two thousand acres are lost through erosion, but the amount of cultivable land has gone up from five thousand to eight thousand.

the self-defenses of the poor.[12] When trade unions insist on job security for their members, they don't have the interests of the firm in mind. Yet as an unintended consequence lower turnover rates increase productivity, by lowering training and recruitment costs.[13] Mechanisms such as these are the stuff of social science.

A long-standing puzzle in the philosophy of social explanation is whether unintended consequences can enter into the explanation of the action or actions that caused them. In an obvious sense, they cannot. To explain an action we must appeal to some event that preceded it in time. The future cannot bring about the past. We can ask the question differently, however, with respect to a pattern or sequence of actions rather than a single action. In that case, could the unintended consequences of something I do today explain why I also do it tomorrow?[14]

Chance variation with subsequent selection is one way in which this could happen. In social life, artificial rather than natural selection is the most plausible mechanism. The pattern of research activities, for instance, is explained largely by benefits desired by the funding institutions but not intended by scientists. Many scientists routinely search funding from the Department of Defense, to carry out work motivated by purely intellectual concerns.[15] The Department of Defense, presumably, funds the applications that are judged to have the greatest military potential. The resulting allocation of research funds is explained by consequences that are incidental from the scientists' point of view.

Reinforcement provides another mechanism by which un-

---

12 One could say that the rich were hoist by their own petard, as poverty was due largely to exploitation by landlords. It was an effect of exploitation that by pure accident generated a counterweight to exploitation.

13 It is not clear that firms should welcome unions, however, since they also tend to get higher wages for their members.

14 We may restrict ourselves to consequences that are in some sense beneficial. The benefits need not, however, accrue to the agents themselves, as shown by the research funding example in the text.

15 Much work in pure linguistics, for instance, has been funded by the U.S. Navy Signal Corps.

intended consequences could explain the persistence of the behavior that causes them. The first temper tantrum occurs, let us suppose, because the child is frustrated by not getting something he wants, such as some ice cream. After a while, he gets the ice cream, which is what he wanted. He also gets something more important, which was no part of his intention – the attention of his parents. Somehow – we don't know how – the gratification from being paid attention becomes associated with the tantrum behavior and reinforces it. Still, getting attention never becomes the intended goal of the child's behavior.

When sociologists explain behavior by unintended consequences, they usually have in mind neither selection nor reinforcement. Unfortunately, it is hard to tell what they do have in mind. A much-discussed example is the rain dance performed in certain societies. The dance doesn't bring rain, but it brings something more important: social cohesion and solidarity. In our societies, church going can have much the same effect or, as many sociologists would claim, *function*. To say that the function of ritual is to maintain social cohesion is to say more than that ritual has that effect. It is to claim that the effect explains the ritual. Now, it is hard to get the facts right in such cases. Social cohesion is difficult to measure. Yet assuming that we could somehow establish that social cohesion is enhanced by these rituals, how would we go about the next step – explaining ritual in terms of the unintended contribution to social cohesion?

Since the notion of social cohesion is so elusive anyway, another example may be more helpful. One might think that overt conflict within an organization is bad for its efficiency. Yet the alternative may be worse. If all conflict is suppressed, tension accumulates until one day the organization breaks down. It is much better if the members can let off small puffs of steam at regular intervals than to have the whole engine explode. Can we conclude, therefore, that the *function* of conflict is to keep the organization in good shape and that conflict is explained by that unintended consequence?

The following mechanism could support an affirmative answer. An organization that does not allow conflict is unstable. After a while it will break down and arise in new, modified form. Either the new form allows conflict or it doesn't. If it does, it is viable and can be expected to remain in place for some time. If it doesn't, it will break down again. Sooner or later, a stable form will arise. If we find that most existing organizations do allow conflict, the explanation is that those who don't are unstable and unlikely to be heavily represented in the population of organizations. The argument would not explain why any particular organization allows conflict, but it would explain why a preponderance of them do so. And it would explain that fact in terms of an unintended, useful consequence of conflict.

This argument is a bit like the argument from social selection discussed in chapter VIII and vulnerable to a similar objection. To work, the process of adaptation has to be quite rapid compared with the rate of change of the environment. The latter depends on two things: the rate at which new organizations are being created and the rate at which old organizations become obsolete. The speed of adaptation also depends on two factors: the time it takes for an unstable organization to break down and the likelihood that the successor of an unstable organization will be stable. In complex, modern societies the environment could well change so rapidly that the process of adaptation has little chance of catching up.

XI

EQUILIBRIUM

EARLIER I said that the social sciences have to explain why we are not in the state of nature. Another challenge is to explain why societies have a modicum of *order* – why they do not offer "a tale told by an idiot, full of sound and fury, signifying nothing." This phrase from *Macbeth* evokes a different kind of anarchy than that suggested by Hobbes's description of life in the state of nature, as "solitary, poor, nasty, brutish and short." It conveys a lack of coordination rather than a lack of cooperation, chaos rather than nastiness. In the preceding chapter we looked at some ways in which people's plans can be thwarted. But no society could work if everybody's plans were thwarted all the time. Universal frustration of plans would be chaos.

Each problem – why we are not in the state of nature and why we are not in a state of chaos – could be resolved in two ways. On the one hand, cooperation and coordination may emerge by decentralized, uncoerced action. This is the topic of this chapter and the two following ones. On the other hand, cooperation and coordination may be centrally imposed by social institutions backed by force. This is the topic of chapter XV, where I also argue, however, that the distinction is less clear-cut than it might appear.

The meaning of equilibrium in the social sciences is a state in which people's plans are consistent with each other. Usually, but not invariably, this also ensures that unintended consequences will not occur. In Fig. X.2, equilibrium is where the supply and demand curves cross. If hog farmers expect the equilibrium price to obtain next year, they will make decisions (about how much to produce) which cause that price to be realized.

101

A simpler example is provided by rules of the road. If I expect everyone else to drive on the right-hand side of the road, it is in my interest to do so as well. This suggests a definition of equilibrium. Consider some number of people, all with their desires and opportunities, and suppose that each decides to take some action. When all have carried out their decisions, each person can ask himself the following question. Given what the others did, could I have done better for myself by acting otherwise? In equilibrium, each person would answer no. Everybody driving on the right-hand side of the road is an equilibrium, because nobody has an incentive to act otherwise. Similarly, when all farmers act on the assumption that the equilibrium price will be realized none of them will regret it.

The traffic equilibrium has some features that other equilibria lack. If everyone drives on the right-hand side of the road, I have no incentive to act otherwise – nor would I wish anyone else to act otherwise. Many equilibria do not have the latter feature. Each farmer would like his rivals to produce less than the equilibrium volume, because this will send prices, and his profits, up.[1] Equilibria with the property that nobody would want anyone to act otherwise are called *convention equilibria*. Linguistic conventions are a prominent example. Because I want to be understood I have an incentive to speak correctly, and because I want to understand what others say I would like them to do so too. Among Mafia leaders in New York, there is a convention to dine out with one's mistress on Fridays and with one's wife on Saturdays, to avoid embarrassing encounters. Knowing that others follow this practice, I will do so myself, to avoid meeting their wives when I dine out with my mistress and vice versa. For the same reason I would want them to follow it too. Once established, these equilibria are extremely robust.

The choice between driving on the right-hand or left-hand side of the road is one with *multiple equilibria*, since countries

---

1 If they do, however, he will regret that he did not produce more.

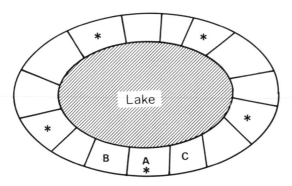

Figure XI.1

where everyone drives on the left are also in equilibrium. (The hog producers, by contrast, have only one equilibrium.) Now, it isn't really important which equilibrium is chosen on the road. As long as everyone does the same, it doesn't matter what they do. In other cases, it can matter a great deal which equilibrium is realized. In easy cases, one equilibrium is preferred by everybody. In hard cases, some prefer one, while others would like another to come about.

To illustrate I return to the example of deforestation (Fig. XI.1). There are a number of peasant plots around a lake. I shall tell three stories about different choices the peasants could be facing. In the first story, deforestation has occurred and erosion is underway. It can be stopped, however, if new trees are planted. Specifically, erosion can be stopped on an individual plot such as *A* if and only if trees are planted on that plot and on both the adjoining plots, *B* and *C*. There are two equilibria. In one, no trees are planted and the land is lost to the lake. No individual peasant can do anything to stop it. In the other, trees are planted on all plots and erosion is halted. Given that others cooperate in reforestation, it is in the interest of each to go along. This equilibrium, although better for all than the first, may not be realized. The peasants may not know that their situation is as I have described it. But if they do (and know that others do), they will agree on a policy of reforestation.[2]

In the second story, agreement is harder to realize. In this story we stipulate that erosion occurs on a given plot if and only if trees are cut down on that plot and on both adjacent plots. Now, there are three equilibria. Each of them requires peasants on every third plot – for instance, all the plots with asterisks in Fig. XI.1, to abstain from felling trees. Peasants on the plots with asterisks do not have an incentive to fell trees, because in that case they would bring about erosion on their own plot. Peasants on plots without asterisks do not have an incentive to abstain, since they risk nothing by felling trees on their plot. All peasants are better off if one of these equilibria is realized than if deforestation occurs on all plots. The question is, who shall be allowed to get more land and who shall sacrifice themselves for the others? Information is not enough: bargaining or coercion is needed.

The second story differs from the rules of the road in another way too. Each traffic equilibrium requires everybody to behave in the same way – everybody should drive on the right or everybody should drive on the left. Each equilibrium in the second story requires that some people behave differently than others – not because their desires or opportunities differ, but because there is a built-in imbalance in their interaction. This is also a feature of "frequency-dependent equilibria," which I referred to in chapter I. Consider the problem of whether it pays to behave honestly in order to build a reputation for honesty. In a population that consisted almost entirely of honest people, it would

---

2 These are not convention equilibria. The case of two convention equilibria, one of which is preferred by everybody over the other, is illustrated by the problem of what to do when a phone call is interrupted. If both parties try to call up again, both will get a busy signal. If neither tries, the outcome will be equally bad. Either of two conventions could ensure equilibrium: the party who made the first call could be designated as the one to call up again, or the party who received the first call could be so designated. Of these, the first is superior, since the party who made the first call would be sure to know what number to call, whereas the receiving party might not know what number the other person had called from. As far as I know, however, there is no convention regulating this situation.

not pay to gather information about people's reputation. Since cheating would go undetected and unpunished, a single cheater would fare better than the honest persons. If, however, much cheating were going on, a person could do better for himself by building a reputation for honesty. In equilibrium, some will behave honestly and others dishonestly. Once again, the argument is not that people differ from each other in intrinsic ways – only that in equilibrium they will behave differently.

Each traffic equilibrium is better for everyone than any other pattern of behavior. In the first erosion story, one equilibrium is *worse* for everyone, that, namely, in which no reforestation is undertaken. Fortunately, there is also another equilibrium, which is preferred by everybody to anything else they could do. In the Prisoner's Dilemma, there is only one equilibrium, which is worse for everybody than a cooperative (nonequilibrium) pattern. We can illustrate this case by a third erosion story, in which we suppose that erosion occurs on a given plot if and only if trees are cut down on both adjoining plots. Whatever others do, it is in the interest of the individual peasant to fell trees on his plot, since in doing that he harms only his neighbors, not himself. The equilibrium outcome is that the land is lost to the lake, unless a political solution is found.

The Prisoner's Dilemma equilibrium differs from all the other equilibria mentioned so far, in that it is made up of actions each of which is the best response to *anything* others could do, not just to their equilibrium behavior. Equilibrium then does not require a person to have correct expectations about what others will do, since he will take the same action whatever he expects them to do. (An action of this type is called a *dominant strategy.*) If he expects wrongly, he will be surprised, perhaps unpleasantly so, but he will not regret what he did. In such cases there can be unintended consequences in equilibrium. Usually, however, surprise and regret go together.

The equilibria discussed in the preceding paragraph are very robust. The only thing that might perturb them is some irrational action. At the other extreme is a class of very fragile equilibria – so fragile, in fact, that they are unlikely to be realized. They have the peculiar property that each person can choose *any* action as the best response to the equilibrium behavior of others. *All* responses are best responses. It doesn't matter what he does, as long as others stick to the equilibrium. But why should they? Rational-choice theory is indeterminate at equilibrium.

To explain this class of equilibria, we must refine the concept of rational action. So far, acting rationally has been understood as carrying out a *well-defined action* that maximizes the agent's utility. Sometimes, however, it is rational to act randomly – to set up a chance device that attaches a *well-defined probability* to each action in the opportunity set, and then let the flip of a coin or the toss of a die decide which will actually be carried out. What is maximized here is not the utility of the action that is finally executed, but the average utility of all actions.

Consider the game of "Chicken," a well-known ritual from American juvenile culture. Two boys drive their cars toward each other, and the first to swerve, or "chicken out," has lost. Suppose the payoffs are as follows:

Paul	Peter	
	Swerves	Does not swerve
Swerves	3, 3	0, 6
Does not swerve	6, 0	−6, −6

We at once see two equilibria. In each, one player swerves and the other does not. In addition, there is a third equilibrium, in which each player decides to swerve with $\frac{2}{3}$ probability. Look at the situation from Paul's point of view. He expects Peter to swerve with probability $\frac{2}{3}$. What is his best response? With what probability p should *he* decide to swerve?[3] His expected utility

3 This includes the possibility that p equals 1 or 0.

depends on his utility in the four possible outcomes, weighted by their probability of occurring. The probability of both swerving is $\frac{2}{3} \cdot p$.[4] The probability of Paul swerving and Peter not swerving is $\frac{1}{3} \cdot p$. The probability of Paul not swerving and Peter swerving is $\frac{2}{3}(1 - p)$. The probability of neither swerving is $\frac{1}{3}(1 - p)$. Matching probabilities with utilities, Paul's expected utility is equal to $\frac{2}{3} \cdot p \cdot 3 + \frac{1}{3} \cdot p \cdot 0 + \frac{2}{3}(1 - p) \cdot 6 + \frac{1}{3}(1 - p) \cdot -6 = 2$. If Peter swerves with the equilibrium probability $\frac{2}{3}$, Paul gets 2 whatever he does![5] In particular, he gets 2 if he swerves with the equilibrium probability $\frac{2}{3}$.

But why should he do that? Since rational behavior is indeterminate in equilibrium, it cannot be sustained by rational considerations.[6] And it is hard to see what else could sustain it. It is highly fragile. Not infrequently, all equilibria are of this sort. The research and development game discussed in chapter IV is an illustration. In equilibrium, all firms use a randomizing device to decide how much to invest in research and development. It does not take much knowledge of actual firms to discredit that idea as a description of what they do. Firms must make a decision, one way or another, but we would not expect their decisions to be best responses to each other.

I have discussed what it means to be in equilibrium and surveyed various types of equilibria. But I have not so far given any reasons to expect an equilibrium to emerge except in the special case of equilibria made up of dominant strategies. Several questions must be addressed. If we begin out of equilibrium, is there a mechanism that sooner or later will bring us to an equilib-

---

4 This invokes a principle used earler, that the probability of two independent events both happening is the product of the probability of each of them occurring.

5 The general theorem illustrated here is that, if the equilibrium behavior of an agent is to choose one of several actions with nonzero probability, he can do no worse (and, by definition of an equilibrium, no better) for himself by choosing any other probability mix of these same actions, including the case of choosing one of them with 100% probability.

6 Paul knows, of course, that the same argument applies to Peter. So there is really no reason he should expect Peter to use the equilibrium probability either. And this makes it even more pointless for him to stick to it.

rium? If there are several equilibria, which, if any, will be realized? If an equilibrium is realized, is it stable against small perturbations? Against large perturbations?

In the cobweb cycle, as drawn in Fig. X.2, the equilibrium is unstable. Any small perturbation will set up an ever-widening cycle. By the same token, if the farmers begin out of equilibrium, they will never come near it. If we draw the diagram differently, with the supply curve steeper than the demand curve, the opposite is true. After a while, the farmers converge to the equilibrium and return to it after any accidental perturbation. A preliminary conclusion might be that the realization of an equilibrium depends on details of the interaction. Some deviations from equilibrium correct themselves, while others get out of hand.

Yet this conclusion has been challenged. Consider the explosive cobweb cycle. One line of argument is that after a while the farmers will begin to form their price expectations in a more sophisticated way. Instead of looking merely at this year's price, they will take account of last year's as well, predicting that next year's will be an average of current and past prices. This learning mechanism, usually referred to as *adaptive expectations,* makes it more likely that equilibrium will be attained.[7] But then we encounter an old problem: in a rapidly changing world, learning and adaptation may be an inefficient mechanism for attaining equilibrium. By the time the farmers figure out what is going on, technology and consumer tastes may have changed so much that past prices are irrelevant.

Another line of argument is to stipulate *rational expectations.* In essence, this means that persons living in a society use the same models and the same information as the social scientist studying them. If he can anticipate what will happen, so can they. To achieve equilibrium, farmers do not have to go through a long sequence of cycles and learning. Using the cobweb model, they

7 This is not evident, but it can be demonstrated.

instantaneously perceive what the equilibrium price must be and act accordingly.

There are many arguments for the rational-expectations hypothesis. In the simple cobweb cycle, and even with adaptive expectations, we must assume that each agent believes himself to be the only one to adjust rationally to the circumstances and that others act in a more or less mechanical way.[8] But this is an irrational belief, which we should not impute to people without evidence. It is surely more plausible to assume that people believe others to be as rational as themselves. Also, in a rapidly changing world people would be silly to pay much attention to the past. When oil prices quadrupled in 1973, the prices of oil before 1973 lost all relevance as guides to future prices. And if ordinary people understood much less of the economy than economists do, we would expect the latter to make much more money than they in fact do. The reason economists don't make a killing by outguessing the market is that the market has access to whatever information they have and can use it just as efficiently.[9]

An obvious objection to these claims is that, in the face of unemployment, stock market crashes and the like, it is wildly implausible to say that people are making correct guesses about what will happen. Surely, these consequences cannot have been fully foreseen. Rational-expectation theorists respond by saying that anticipations are more complex. People do not anticipate future events as if they were certain to happen. Rather, they form probability estimates over the many future events that can happen. These estimates are rational, in the sense of taking account of all available information and not being subject to systematic

8 This is seen very clearly in the bandwagon – underdog example of chapter X but is also true of the cobweb cycle. When a farmer believes that prices will remain constant from this year to the next, this makes sense only on the assumption that other people will behave next year as they have this year.
9 Two rational-expectation economists are walking down Wall Street. One of them sees a fifty-dollar bill on the sidewalk and bends down to pick it up. The other stops him by saying that if the bill was genuine someone would have picked it up already.

biases, but they are not infallible. If a low-probability event comes to pass, people will be surprised and perhaps disappointed, but it is not as if the outcome were totally unforeseen. In fact, the most improbable event would be that improbable events never occurred. Unemployment and stock market crashes *are* equilibrium phenomena, since nobody, looking back at the actions that caused them, can say that they did something that, in light of what was known to them at the time, they should not have done. This response presupposes, however, that the process of forming subjective probabilities is reliable. I argued in chapter IV that often it is not.

Multiple equilibria pose a formidable problem for the rational-expectations argument. A convention equilibrium like rules of the road cannot emerge by rational expectations, if the situation offers no clue to what others will do.[10] (I shall have more to say about clues later.) Multiple equilibria with different winners and losers, as in the second version of the erosion story, are even less hospitable to rational expectations. In this circumstance many things might happen. The situation might remain indefinitely out of equilibrium. The realization of one equilibrium rather than another could happen by accident. One set of individuals might be sufficiently powerful to impose the equilibrium that favored them over other people. What can be ruled out is the realization of one equilibrium by tacit coordination and rational anticipation.

If we look beyond rational expectations to psychological cues, tacit coordination becomes easier. In logic, there is no difference between left and right. In reality, right has a psychological dominance or salience because most people are right-handed. If two persons are told that they have to designate either right or left, and that both will be rewarded if they make the same choice,

---

10 By contrast, the convention that the person who made the first telephone call should be the one to call again if the conversation is interrupted could emerge by rational expectations. The fact that there is no such convention counts against the rational-expectations theory, but since the problem is not very important it is not a powerful counterexample.

both will choose right even when there is no possibility of communication. Or suppose they are told they can win a thousand dollars if they make claims on it that add up to exactly that amount, in which case each will get what he claimed. Any pair of numbers that adds up to a thousand is an equilibrium. One pair stands out, however: each claims five hundred. Almost everyone makes this choice when given the occasion.

I said that equilibria can emerge by accident. Suppose that there are two competing conventions for regulating behavior at crossroads. One says that drivers coming from the left should yield, the other that drivers on minor roads should yield.[11] If there happen to be more drivers adhering to the first convention than to the second, those who follow the first will on the average have fewer accidents.[12] Some followers of the second will notice this and switch to the first, thereby making it even more advantageous (and its advantages even more likely to be noticed), until in the end everybody follows the first. (Or the mechanism could emerge by accident in a more literal and more gruesome sense, if people who follow the second convention are eliminated in the traffic accidents to which they are disproportionately prone.) The second convention could also have become dominant, however, if it had been more frequently followed in the first place.

Finally, an equilibrium can be imposed by those who stand to benefit most from it. To do so, they need leverage over those who prefer another equilibrium. Often, the leverage is that those who have the most to gain also have the least to lose. This statement is less paradoxical than it appears, since two comparisons are involved. For the weak, law and order is very important, even if it is heavily biased against them. Without law and

---

11 I assume that it is always clear which road is minor and which is major.
12 Followers of either convention do better than people who never yield. If both conventions have a substantial number of followers, they do worse, however, than people who always yield. To get around this difficulty, we could suppose that most people are irrationally impatient and unwilling to use the always-yield strategy.

order – in the state of nature – they would not survive. The strong also prefer law and order to the state of nature, and they naturally prefer law and order biased in their favor over law and order favoring the weak. Nevertheless, because they are strong, they could survive in the state of nature. There is less at stake for the strong, which is another way of saying that they have more bargaining power, which they can use to impose their preferred equilibrium. I say more about this in chapter XIV.

A disastrous legacy from the biological approach to society (chapter VIII) is the assumption that societies are stable. On this view, any departure from equilibrium sets in motion forces that reestablish it, much as any deviation from the normal bodily temperature triggers off processes (sweating or shivering) that bring it back to normal. Consider the cobweb cycle in this perspective. Some disequilibria are eliminated by simple convergence to the equilibrium. If the process does not converge (as in Fig. X.2) adaptive expectations will stabilize it. If that does not work either, political action will do it. Societies are not like organisms, however. There is no reason to think them so wonderfully designed that any deviation from equilibrium is automatically canceled.

XII

SOCIAL NORMS

RATIONAL action – be it economically or politically motivated – is concerned with outcomes. Rationality says, "If
you want to achieve *Y*, do *X*." Action guided by social norms
is not outcome-oriented. The simplest social norms are of the
type "Do *X*" or "Don't do *X*." More complex norms have a
conditional form: "If you do *Y*, then do *X*," or "If others do *Y*,
then do *X*." An even more complex norm says, "If it would be
good if all did *X*, then do *X*." For such norms to be *social*, they
must be shared by other people and partly sustained by their
approval and disapproval. Typically, they are also sustained by
the emotions that are triggered when they are violated: embar-
rassment, guilt and shame in the violator; anger and indignation in the observers. Frequently, a norm to do *X* is accompa-
nied by a higher-level norm to punish those who violate the
first-order norm, where the punishment can range from raised
eyebrows to social ostracism.

This characterization of social norms is controversial, more so
perhaps than most other arguments in this book. I shall discuss
objections later, but first we need some illustrations of what I
have in mind when I talk about social norms. I shall focus on
the issue of whether social norms serve an ulterior purpose, that
is, whether they are in some sense useful for the individual or
for the society. When they are, we should not conclude, without further argument, that they exist *because* they serve that
purpose.

Some norms are a bit like conventions, except that it is not
clear that any ulterior purpose is being served. Norms of dress,
rules of etiquette and dietary rules fall in this category. Some-

times these norms are compared to traffic rules, but a moment's reflection shows that the analogy is misleading. If I violate a traffic rule, two bad things can happen to me. I can get into an accident, and I may be blamed by bystanders, because bad things can happen to them if I drive recklessly. If I pick up the wrong fork at the dinner table, the only bad thing that can happen to me is that others will blame me for my bad manners. But why would they do this? They suffer no harm or risk if I pick up the wrong fork. They might be blamed, however, if they did not blame me.

Other social norms take the form of codes of honor. Many societies have strict rules of vengeance, with vendettas going on for generations. Revenge is not guided by the prospect of future gain but triggered by an earlier offense. Although the propensity to take revenge is not guided by consequences, it can have good consequences. If other people believe that I invariably take revenge for an offense, even at great risk to myself, they will take care not to offend me. If they believe that I will react to offense only when it is in my interest to react, they need not be as careful. From the rational point of view, a threat is not credible unless it will be in the interest of the threatener to carry it out when the time comes. The threat to kill oneself, for instance, is not rationally credible. Threats backed by a code of honor are very effective, since they will be executed even if it is in the interest of the threatener not do so. So it might appear as if an ulterior purpose is being served by the code, although the person abiding by it is not motivated by an ulterior purpose. Noninstrumental action can be instrumentally useful. Yet a moment's reflection shows that this case is an exception. When a person guided by a code of honor has a quarrel with one who is exclusively motivated by rational considerations, the first will often have his way. In a quarrel between two persons guided by the code, both may do worse than if they had agreed to let the legal system resolve their conflict.[1] Since we are talking about

---

1 This may be why Mafiosi do better in the United States than in Sicily.

codes of honor that are shared social norms, the latter case is the typical one.

There are norms regulating what money can buy. For instance, there seems to be a social norm against walking up to a person in a cinema queue and asking to buy his place.[2] Note that nobody would be harmed by this practice. Other people in the line would not lose their place. The person asked to sell his place would be free to refuse. If he accepted, both he and the buyer would gain by the exchange. It has been suggested that the norm is a special case of a more general norm against flaunting one's wealth, a norm that serves the ulterior purpose of reducing envy and conflict. But this norm operates within a community of people who know one another, not among strangers waiting in line. There is no norm against standing in line with expensive furs or jewelry, although such behavior is also a way of flaunting one's wealth.

For another example, consider a suburban community where all houses have small lawns of the same size. Suppose a house-owner is willing to pay his neighbor's son ten dollars to mow his lawn, but not more. He would rather spend half an hour mowing the lawn himself than pay eleven dollars to have someone else do it. Imagine now that the same person is offered twenty dollars to mow the lawn of another neighbor. It is easy to imagine that he would refuse, probably with some indignation. But this has an appearance of irrationality. By turning down the offer of having his neighbor's son mow his lawn for eleven dollars, he implies that half an hour of his time is worth at most eleven dollars. By turning down the offer to mow the other neighbor's lawn for twenty dollars, he implies that it is worth at least twenty dollars. But it cannot both be worth less than eleven and be worth more than twenty dollars.

As an explanation, it has been suggested that people evaluate losses and gains foregone differently. Credit card companies exploit this difference when they insist that stores advertise cash

2 I have asked several hundred people if they believe there is such a norm. Only about 5% have said that in their opinion there is not.

discounts rather than credit card surcharges. The credit card holder is affected less by the lost chance of getting the cash discount than by the extra cost of paying with the card. Similarly, the houseowner is affected more by the out-of-pocket expenses that he would incur by paying someone to mow his lawn than by the loss of a windfall income. But this cannot be the full story, because it does not explain why the houseowner should be indignant at the proposal. Part of the explanation must be that he doesn't think of himself as the kind of person who mows other people's lawns for money. It *isn't done*, to use a revealing phrase that often accompanies social norms. Here it is plausible that an ulterior purpose is being served. Social relations among neighbors would be disturbed if differences in wealth were too blatantly displayed and if some of them treated others as salaried employees. Yet on any given occasion that is usually not the reason or motive for refusing the offer, or for not making it. It simply isn't done.

An important set of norms tell people to cooperate in Prisoner's Dilemma types of situations. Norms of voting are an important example, among many others. It is better for almost everybody if most people vote, because otherwise democracy might be undermined and give way to an authoritarian regime. For any individual, however, there is little point in voting, since his influence on the viability of democracy is almost nil. And yet most people vote in democratic societies. In chapter VI various explanations were considered, in terms of altruism, Kantianism and fairness. Of these, the last two are social norms as I use that term here.[3] Kantianism tells people to do X, if X is an activity that would benefit all if all engaged in it. It is not outcome-oriented and may in fact have bad consequences. If some but not all engage in the activity that would benefit all if all engaged in it, everybody might be worse off than they would be if nobody engaged in it. Unilateral disarmament could, under some

3 Altruism, or a more impersonal version of it, could be a *moral norm* (chapter VI).

circumstances, be an example. The norm of fairness tells people to do X if most other people do X, if one benefits from their doing X and if one would benefit from not doing X. It is a norm against free riding. But it is not outcome-oriented, since it enjoins a person to cooperate even when everybody would be better off if he took a free ride.

There is no question that these norms serve an ulterior purpose. Even if on any given occasion they may work against the general interest, these cases are infrequent. On the whole, they are immensely beneficial. Civilization as we know it would not exist without them. But that is not to say that people act to maintain civilization when they follow these norms. Once again, noninstrumental norms can have instrumentally useful consequences. The noninstrumental norm of revenge has useful consequences for the individual who follows it, but only if nobody else does. The norms of cooperation have useful consequences for other people, at least under most circumstances. The details of the argument are spelled out in the next chapter.

Sometimes people will invoke a social norm to rationalize self-interest. Suppose my wife and I are having a dinner party for eight and that four persons have already been invited. We discuss whether to invite a particular couple for the last two places and find ourselves in disagreement, for somewhat murky reasons. I like the woman of the couple, and my wife doesn't like it that I like her. But we don't want to state these reasons. Instead we appeal to social norms. I invoke the norm of reciprocity, saying, "Since they had us over for dinner, it is our turn to invite them now." My wife invokes another norm: "Since we have already invited two single men, we must invite two women, to create a balance."

In wage negotiations, sheer bargaining power (chapter XIV) counts for much. Appeal to accepted social norms can also have some efficacy, however. To justify wage increases, workers can refer to the earning power of the firm, the wage level in other firms or occupations, the percent wage increase in other firms or occupations and the absolute wage increases in other firms or occupations. When changes are being compared, they can choose the reference year so as to make their own case as strong as possible. Employers use similar arguments to resist claims for wage increases. Each argument can be supported by a norm of fair wages. There is a norm of fair division of the surplus between capital and labor. Employers will appeal to this norm when the firm does badly, workers when it does well. There is a norm of equal pay for equal work. Workers will appeal to this norm when they earn less than workers in similar firms, but not when they earn more. The norm of preservation of status, or wage differences, can also be exploited for bargaining purposes.

Some argue that this is all there is to norms: they are tools of manipulation, used to dress up self-interest in more acceptable garb. But this cannot be true. Some norms, like the norm of vengeance, obviously override self-interest. A more general argument against the cynical view of norms is that, if nobody believed in norms, there would be nothing to manipulate. Colin Turnbull's description of norm manipulation among the Ik, cited in chapter VI, is an excellent example. If some people successfully exploit norms for self-interested purposes, it can only be because others are willing to let norms take precedence over self-interest. Moreover, even those who appeal to the norm usually believe in it, or else the appeal might not have much power. The power of norms derives from the emotional tonality that gives them a grip on the mind. Faking emotion is possible, but the real thing is more convincing.

The would-be manipulator of norms is also constrained by the need to be consistent. Even if the norm has no grip on his mind, he must act as if it did. Having invoked the norm of reciprocity on one occasion, I cannot just dismiss it when my wife appeals to it on another occasion. An employer may successfully appeal to the workers and get them to share the burdens in a bad year. The cost he pays is that in a good year he may also have to share the benefits. By making the earlier appeal, he has committed himself to the norm of a fair division of the surplus.

It is time to face an obvious objection to my account of norms, and in particular to the claim that norm-guided behavior is not outcome-oriented. When people obey norms, they often have a particular outcome in mind: they want to avoid the disapproval of other people. Norm-guided behavior is supported by the threat of social sanctions that make it rational to obey the norms. Suppose I face the choice between taking revenge for an insult to my sister and not doing anything. The cost of revenge is that I might in turn be the target of countervengeance. The cost of not doing anything is that my family and friends are certain to desert me, leaving me out on my own, defenselessly exposed to predators. A cost–benefit analysis might well tell me that revenge is the rational choice. The countervengeance is uncertain, since it might be directed toward another member of my family, clan or tribe. The consequences of remaining passive, by contrast, are certain.

In response to this argument, we can first observe that norms do not need external sanctions to be effective. When norms are *internalized,* they are followed even when violation would be unobserved and not exposed to sanctions. Shame or anticipation of it is a sufficient internal sanction. I don't pick my nose when I can be observed by people on a train passing by, even if I am confident that they are all perfect strangers whom I shall never see again and who have no power to impose sanctions on me. I don't throw litter in the park, even when there is nobody around to observe me. If punishment were nothing but the price of crime, nobody would feel shame when caught. In the process of internalizing norms other people's attitudes are essential, but once the process has been achieved the norms stand, as it were, on their own. It will not do to argue that following the norm even when unobserved is a rational way of economizing on decision costs. Sometimes one knows that one would have much to gain and nothing to lose from violating a norm – nothing, that is, except self-respect. This is not to say that sanctions are superfluous once a norm has been internalized. Human nature being what it is, external sanctions are a useful counterweight to weakness of will.

We must also ask why people would sanction others for violating norms. What's in it for them? One answer could be that, if they do not express their disapproval of the violation, they will themselves be the target of disapproval by third parties.[4] When there is a norm to do X, there is often, as I said, a higher-order norm to sanction people who fail to do X. And there might even be a norm to sanction people who fail to sanction people who fail to do X. As long as the cost of expressing disapproval is less than the cost of receiving disapproval for not expressing it, it is in one's rational self-interest to express it. Now, expressing disapproval is always costly, whatever the target behavior. At the very least it requires energy and attention that might be used for other purposes. One may alienate or provoke the target individual, at some cost or risk to oneself. On the other hand, when one moves upward in the chain of actions, beginning with the original violation, the cost of receiving disapproval falls rapidly to zero. People do not frown upon others when they fail to sanction people who fail to sanction people who fail to sanction people who fail to sanction a norm violation. Consequently, some sanctions must be performed for motives other than the fear of being sanctioned. I argued in the preceding paragraph that sometimes there is an unmoved mover at the very beginning of the chain. Here I have argued that every chain must have one.[5]

Even if consequences are not part of the proximate motivation of norm-guided behavior, they might still enter into the explanation of norms. Norms might exist because they are useful for the individual or for the group that follows them. Now, some of the norms that I have mentioned are unquestionably useful, such as the norms of cooperation. The usefulness of the others is more doubtful.

---

4 They might even be the target of disapproval by the first party – the person, that is, whose violations they fail to sanction. The reader is encouraged to think of examples!

5 In the language of the preceding chapter, if norm-guided behavior is sustained only by external sanctions, it is not an equilibrium.

Rules of etiquette, norms of dress and the like do not seem to have any useful consequences. On the contrary, the rigid grip of these norms on the mind seems to create a great deal of pointless misery. It is sometimes argued that they serve the useful function of confirming one's identity or membership in a social group. This claim is a bit like the rain-dance argument mentioned in chapter X. Since the notion of social identity is elusive, it is hard to evaluate. A weakness of the argument is that it does not explain why these rules are as complicated as they often are. To signal or confirm one's membership in a group one sign should be sufficient, like the wearing of a badge or a tie. Instead, there is often vast redundancy. The manner of speaking of an Oxford-educated person differs from standard spoken English in many more ways than what is required to single him out as an Oxford graduate. One reply is that the complexity of the rules serves an additional function, that of keeping outsiders out and upstarts down. It is easy to imitate one form of behavior, but hard to learn a thousand subtly different rules. But that argument flounders on the fact that working-class life is no less norm-regulated than that of the upper classes. Whereas many middle-class persons would like to pass themselves off as members of the upper class, few try to pass themselves off as workers.[6]

Norms of vengeance are also ambiguous in this respect. One could argue that there will be fewer quarrels in societies regulated by codes of honor, since everybody will know that they can have disastrous consequences. But it is not clear that this would be a good thing. One could probably eliminate almost all criminal behavior if all crimes carried the death penalty, but the costs of creating this terror regime would be prohibitive. And in any case vendetta-ridden societies have a very high incidence of death by violence.

---

6 To be sure, one might tell a story about this case too. Norms of etiquette are no less difficult to shed than to acquire. Perhaps it is in the interest of the working class as a whole that its members should not find it easy to leave the class, since the first to do so would tend to be its most gifted members and hence its potential leaders.

Norms regulating the role of money are equally ambiguous. I
don't think the norm against buying places in a cinema queue
has useful consequences, although, of course, it might have.
Any economist worth his salt could, given five minutes, tell a
story about the bad things that would happen if we didn't have
this norm. But to tell a story is not to give an argument. The
norm that prevents us from accepting or making offers to mow
other people's lawns for money seems more promising in this
respect. If I am hard up, I may be tempted to accept or solicit an
offer, thinking, correctly, that one transaction cannot matter.
But an unintended consequence of many monetary deals among
neighbors could be the loss of the spontaneous mutual-help behavior that is one of the main benefits of living in a community.
By preventing deals from being made, the norm preserves the
community.

The norm could also have a more disreputable aspect, however. It is true that, if I offer my neighbor money to mow my
lawn, I flaunt my wealth in a way that is disruptive of community. But the norm against flaunting one's wealth may just be a
special case of a higher-order norm: *Don't stick your neck out.*
"Don't think you are better than us, and above all don't behave
in ways that make us think that you think you are better than
us." This norm, which prevails in many small communities, can
have very bad consequences. It can discourage the gifted from
using their talents, and may lead to their being branded as
witches if they nevertheless use them.

The norm against rate busting found at most work places can
be seen in this perspective. The usual explanation of this norm is
that rate busting induces employers to raise standards, so that in
the end all workers lose. The problem with this account is that it
makes employers seem pretty irrational, since it would be in
their interest to dispel the fear of the workers and commit themselves to a preset standard. An alternative account could be one
in terms of social norms, conformism and envy. The overall
impact of the norm of not sticking one's neck out has probably

not been good, although on occasion it may have useful consequences. While preserving community, it stifles progress.

Let us suppose that we have found that a given norm makes everybody better off than they would be without it. There is still a big step to the conclusion that the norm exists *because* it makes everybody better off. Unless we specify the mechanism by which the unintended benefits of norm-guided behavior sustain the norm, this view is sheer unsubstantiated assertion. Natural selection might explain norms of cooperation, although it doesn't help us understand why they vary so much across societies and why they take so many different forms: altruism, duty, fairness. Otherwise, I don't see any plausible candidates for the mechanism by which the beneficial consequences of norms keep them in place. Unfortunately, I cannot propose any other explanation of norms either. Norms, in my view, result from psychological propensities about which we know little. Although I could tell a story or two about how norms might have emerged,[7] I have nothing to say about how they actually did emerge.

7 As noted in chapter VIII, envy could well be favored by natural selection. Some norm-guided behavior is closely related to envy. This could provide one story. Another evolutionary story is that conformism may have been an efficient strategy of survival for our ancestors, although it later became a hindrance to progress. Perhaps this is how the leopard acquired his spots and the Ethiopian his color; and perhaps not.

XIII

COLLECTIVE ACTION

In *Lake Wobegon Days* Garrison Keillor describes Flag Day in his mythical town. Herman, the organizer of the parade, bought a quantity of blue, red and white caps and distributed them to the townspeople so that they could march through the streets as a Living Flag, while he stood on the roof of the Central Building to take a photograph. Right after the war, people were happy to comply, but later they had second thoughts:

> One cause of resentment was the fact that none of them got to see the Flag they were in; the picture in the paper was black and white. Only Herman and Mr. Hanson got to see the real Flag, and some boys too short to be needed down below. People wanted a chance to go up to the roof and witness the spectacle for themselves.
>
> "How can you go up there if you're supposed to be down here?" Herman said. "You go up there to look, you got nothing to look at. Isn't it enough to know that you're doing your part?"
>
> On Flag Day, 1949, just as Herman said, "That's it! Hold it now!" one of the reds made a break for it – dashed up four flights of stairs to the roof and leaned over and had a long look. Even with the hole he left behind, it was a magnificent sight. The Living Flag filled the street below. A perfect Flag! The reds so brilliant! He couldn't take his eyes off it. "Get down here! We need a picture!" Herman yelled up to him. "How does it look?" people yelled up to him. "Unbelievable! I can't describe it," he said.
>
> So then everyone had to have a look. "No!" Herman said, but they took a vote and it was unanimous. One by one, members of the Living Flag went up to the roof and admired it. It *was* marvelous! It brought tears to the eyes, it made one reflect

on this great country and on Lake Wobegon's place in it all. One wanted to stand up there all afternoon and just drink it in. So, as the first hour passed, and only forty of the five hundred had been to the top, the others got more and more restless. "Hurry up! Quit dawdling! *You've* seen it! Get down here and give someone else a chance!" Herman sent people up in groups of four, and then ten, but after two hours, the Living Flag became the Sitting Flat and then began to erode, as the members who had had a look thought about heading home to supper, which infuriated the ones who hadn't. "Ten more minutes!" Herman cried, but ten minutes became twenty and thirty, and people snuck off and the Flag that remained for the last viewer was a Flag shot through by cannon fire.

In 1950, the Sons of Knute took over Flag Day. Herman gave them the boxes of caps. Since then, the Knutes have achieved several good Flags, though most years the attendance was poor. You need at least four hundred to make a good one. Some years the Knutes made a "no-look" rule, other years they held a lottery. One year they experimented with a large mirror held by two men over the edge of the roof, but when people leaned back and looked up, the Flag disappeared, of course.

The Wobegonians face a collective action problem, albeit an unusual one. Each is tempted to go up on the roof or, in the later experiment, to look into the mirror. But if they all do that, the Flag unravels and there isn't anything to look at.[1] To solve the problem, they resort to classical coordination techniques: to impose a "no-look" rule, to take turns, to have a lottery. The first is not very satisfactory, since there is little point in forming a Flag nobody can see.[2] The others ensure that some people can watch but not so many that there is nothing to watch. They demand, however, centralized coordination, backed by sanctions or at least by authority. In this chapter I discuss decentral-

---

1 One often talks about cooperation "unraveling" through defection. The Living Flag offers a literal illustration of this phrase.
2 God could see it, of course. In medieval cathedrals many wonderful capitals are so high up that nobody can see the details without binoculars, which were not invented when they were built. But since God could see them it didn't matter. The Wobegonians do not seem to have had the same religious fervor.

ized solutions to the collective action problem, reserving central-ized solutions for chapter XV.

Let me define a collective action a bit more carefully. Suppose that each member of a group has the choice between engaging in a certain activity and not engaging in it. The group has a collective action problem if it is better for all if some do it than if nobody does, but better for each not to do it.[3] It may or may not be better for all if all do it than if nobody does. And it may or may not be best if all do it. To *cooperate* is to act against one's self-interest in a way that benefits all if some, or possibly all, act in that way.

In the best-known collective action problem it is best for all if all cooperate. This is an extension of the Prisoner's Dilemma, generalized from two persons to groups of any size. There are innumerable examples in social life of this perverse tendency of individual rationality to generate collective disaster. Here are some examples, to supplement those cited in chapter X.[4] It is better for all workers if all strike for higher wages than if none do, but each worker is better off by remaining on the job. If others strike he reaps the benefit of their effort without paying the cost, and if they don't he can do nothing by himself. It is better for all firms in an industry, or all members of OPEC, if all stick to a production quota or to a cartel price than if all behave competitively, but each has an incentive to break out. It is better for all commuters if all go by bus than if all go by car, but for each it is always better to go by car. It is better for everybody if nobody litters in the park, but individuals have no incentive to abstain from littering. It is better for all firms if all invest in research and development, but in the absence of a patent system it may be better for each firm to borrow from others. Voting, reporting your income correctly, lobbying to keep the local school open, supporting public radio stations and joining a revo-lutionary movement conform to the same pattern.

3 Here "better" means better from the purely self-interested view. "Better for all" is an ambiguous phrase, as will become clear later on.
4 Counterfinality is closely related to the collective action problem.

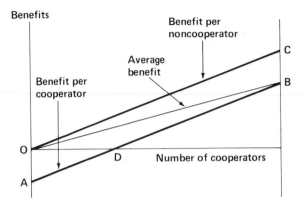

Figure XIII.1

Figure XIII.1 shows the simplest case of the many-person Prisoner's Dilemma. Here the people who do what is best for all if all do it are called cooperators; others are called noncooperators. The two heavy lines show how their expected benefits vary with the number of cooperators.[5] The fact that noncooperation is individually rational, in terms of selfish benefits, is shown by the fact that the line showing reward to noncooperators is consistently above the other. That it is better for all if all cooperate than if none do is shown by the fact that B is above O. As in the two-person Prisoner's Dilemma, the unilateral noncooperator or free rider gets the largest benefit C, whereas the worst outcome A is reserved for the unilateral cooperator. If there are at least D cooperators, they will do better for themselves than if nobody cooperates. The thin line shows how the average benefit for all members in the group, cooperators and noncoopera-

5 There are two ways in which additional cooperators benefit others. They can increase either the amount of a good made available or the probability that it will be made available. When more and more people take the bus to work instead of driving their own car, congestion falls steadily and everybody saves time. When more and more people join a campaign to keep the local school open, the chances that it will succeed get steadily better. Both cases are covered if we think of the benefits as *expected* benefits.

127

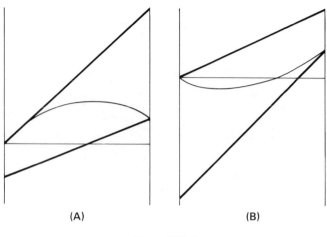

(A) (B)

Figure XIII.2

tors, varies with the number of cooperators. By definition, it must begin at *O* and end at *B*.

The distance between the two curves represents the cost (per cooperator) of cooperation. In the figure the cost does not vary with the number of cooperators, but this is a somewhat atypical case. The cost of cooperation may increase as more people co-operate. As people join call-in campaigns for public radio, the lines become congested and it takes more time to get through. The cost may also decrease: as more people join a revolutionary movement, the government forces have to spread themselves more thinly.

These two cases are shown in Fig. XIII.2, in diagrams A and B, respectively. In case A, the cost of cooperation increases so fast that, as more and more join, the cost exceeds not only the benefit to the cooperator, but the sum total of everybody's bene-fits. This is shown by the fact that the average-benefit curve reaches its highest point when about half of the individuals cooperate. In case B, the cost of cooperation is very high when there are few cooperators. The first cooperators actually make the situation worse.

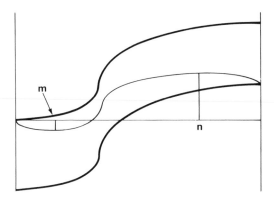

Figure XIII.3

Figures XIII.1 and XIII.2 are atypical in that the benefits of cooperation are shown as constant. Each additional cooperator adds the same amount to everybody's welfare. In reality, the typical situation is that the first and the last contributors add little, whereas those coming in the middle are more efficacious.[6] A few revolutionaries don't do much good, but when almost everyone has joined it makes little difference whether the few who are not committed do so too. Sometimes unanimity is important: a single firm that undersells a cartel can corner the market if it has sufficient productive capacity. Usually, however, a few free riders will not eliminate the benefits.

Figure XIII.3 shows this case, assuming costs of cooperation to be constant. Both phenomena illustrated in diagrams A and B of Fig. XIII.2 are observed. With respect to the average benefit, the cooperators to the left of *m* do more harm than good, as do those to the right of *n*. Now, this phrase is a bit misleading.

6 The phrases "first," "middle" and "last" can refer to the times at which successive cooperators join (as in building a revolutionary movement). But they can also refer to simultaneous acts of cooperation (as in voting). In the latter case, they express a comparison of two situations. To say that the last voters add very little is to say that the benefit created in a situation where everyone votes is very nearly the same as the benefit created when almost everyone votes.

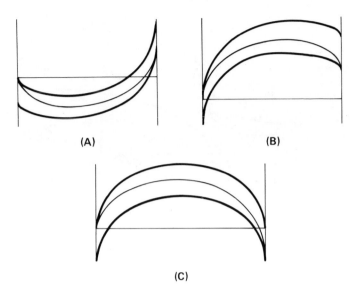

(A)   (B)

(C)

Figure XIII.4

When cooperators do more harm than good, it is because the harm they do to themselves, through the cost of cooperating, exceeds the good they do to everybody else (and to themselves). They don't actually harm other people. Figure XIII.4 illustrates cases in which acts of cooperation *are* positively harmful.

In case A, unilateral acts of cooperation harm everybody. As mentioned in chapter VI, unilateral disarmament illustrates this possibility. Individual acts of rebellion may create a pretext for authorities to crack down not only on the rebels, but on bystanders as well. In case B, the last cooperators partially undo the work of the earlier ones. In chapter VI I gave the example of cleaning up after a party. Or suppose that in wartime everybody insists on joining the army, so that there is nobody left to work in industries that are vital for the war effort. In case C, it is worse for all if all cooperate than if nobody does. We can imagine that after a party there is a great deal of litter on the lawn and that everyone rushes out to pick it up, trampling the lawn in the process. Although not a many-person Prisoner's Dilemma, it is a collective action problem as I have defined it.

Collective action problems arise because it is difficult to get people to cooperate for their mutual benefit. To "solve" the problem is to achieve mutually beneficial cooperation. When universal cooperation is undesirable,[7] a solution must single out who will cooperate and who will not. Solutions can be centralized or decentralized, depending on whether they require externally imposed force and inducements. Decentralized solutions are more basic than centralized ones, since to ensure compliance with a central institution is itself a collective action problem (chapter XV). When, however, universal cooperation is undesirable, it is difficult to single out by a decentralized solution who shall cooperate and who shall not. In such cases, decentralized mechanisms are liable to yield too much cooperation or too little. As in Lake Wobegon, a centralized solution may be necessary. This suggests a two-step process: decentralized collective action with universal participation sets up a central institution with the capacity to enforce selective participation. The relation between strikes and trade unions is a good example. Before workers were organized, it was not possible to direct some of them to strike: it had to be all or none.

Decentralized solutions can come about by a variety of individual motivations: self-interest, altruism, social norms or some combination thereof. There are two mistakes to be avoided in trying to explain cooperative behavior. The crudest is to believe that there exists one privileged motivation – self-interest, for instance – that explains all instances of cooperation. A more subtle error is to believe that each instance of cooperation can be explained by one motivation. In reality, cooperation occurs when and because different motivations reinforce each other.

Self-interest might seem an unlikely motivation, since the collective action problem is defined in part by the clause that it is not selfishly rational to cooperate. And in a one-shot prob-

7 As in diagram A of Fig. XIII.2, in Fig. XIII.3 and in all three diagrams of Fig. XIII.4.

lem this is indeed true. When the same people face collective action problems over and over again, it may be in their self-interest to cooperate, out of hope of reciprocation, fear of retaliation or both. In repeated interactions, each person must choose a *reaction mechanism* that tells him what to do in any given interaction as a function of what he and others did in previous interactions. A particularly simple reaction function, "Tit for Tat," tells people to begin by cooperating in the first round and then to cooperate in any later round if and only if all others cooperated in the previous round. If all adopt this principle, all will cooperate in each interaction. Under certain conditions, universal adoption of Tit for Tat is an equilibrium. If others adopt it, nobody can do better than adopt it himself. Universal adoption of the principle "Never cooperate" is also an equilibrium, but an inferior one.

The conditions under which people will cooperate out of self-interest are quite stringent. The individuals must not be too myopic. To be moved by future retaliation and reciprocation, they must care about the future. If they do, long-term self-interest can substitute for morality or social norms, assuming that some further conditions are satisfied. The gains from universal cooperation must be substantial; the gain from unilateral noncooperation not too large; and the loss from unilateral cooperation small.[8] Finally, each individual must be quite confident that other individuals are rational and fully informed about the situation. Since there is no dominant strategy, he will not adopt Tit for Tat unless he is certain that others will do so too. In large groups, with many people who do not know each other very well, this last condition is unlikely to be realized.[9] Many people, if asked why they cooperate, would probably answer that they do so because others have cooperated in the past, but

8 These statements are approximate, but they can be made precise.
9 In some small, closely knit groups it can be realized. The community of Western bankers apparently manages to hold a united front toward the Third World debtor countries by the belief that a single defection will unravel everything.

this is more likely to reflect a norm of fairness than a reaction mechanism in a self-interested equilibrium.

I believe, therefore, that most cooperation is due to nonselfish motivations of one kind or another. Typically, several motivations coexist and reinforce each other. To illustrate this proposition, let us go back to what I believe is the typical collective action case, depicted in Fig. XIII.3, and suppose that individuals have the various nonselfish motivations discussed in chapter VI. Some are Kantians: they want to do what would be best if all did it. Some are utilitarians: they want to promote the common good. Some are motivated by the norm of fairness: they don't want to take a free ride on the cooperation of others, but neither do they want to cooperate when few others do. There are never many Kantians, but suppose there are as many as m. As long as the number of other cooperators is between m and n, a utilitarian would also want to cooperate, since in that interval each additional act of cooperation would increase the average benefit. The Kantians could act as a trigger or catalyst for utilitarian behavior, and the utilitarians as a multiplier for the Kantians.

The utilitarians might themselves act as a catalyst for people who are motivated by the norm of fairness. For each of the latter, there is some number of other cooperators who will trigger off his cooperation. Some are easily shamed into cooperating, whereas others come around only when almost everyone has joined. For some, the sum total of Kantians and utilitarians may be enough. For others, the sum total of Kantians, utilitarians and those who are triggered off by the sum total of Kantians and utilitarians may be enough. And so on. Depending on the constellation of motivations, the chain reaction may go all the way to universal cooperation or stop short of it. Because the norm of fairness is insensitive to outcomes, there is nothing to stop it from going all the way even if it would be better for all if it did not.

In real life, nobody acts as a utilitarian, if only because it is hard to figure out the shape of the average-benefit curve. But there is evidence that some people have the characteristically utilitarian instinct of cooperating more when others do less, and vice versa.[10] The norm of fairness, of course, points one in exactly the opposite direction. Kantianism by definition is not sensitive to what others do. Next to nothing is known about the distribution of these motivations in the population and the way in which they interact to produce decentralized cooperation.

10 This applies even when decisions are made simultaneously, if simultaneous choices have to be made on many successive occasions. The decision whether to vote in a given election might depend on the turnout in the last election. In this way, political cobweb cycles could be generated.

XIV

BARGAINING

THERE are two types of cooperation. In one, it makes sense to talk about individual acts of cooperation. In the other, the basic unit is a cooperative pattern of behavior – an ensemble of acts of cooperation. Cleaning up litter in the park or paying one's taxes are examples of the first. These are acts that benefit others, even if nobody else cooperates. The Living Flag illustrates the second. If a single individual went out in the street with, say, a red cap on his head, it would not benefit anyone. It takes a substantial number of people to form anything that looks like a flag pattern. This is cooperation in the literal, everyday sense, in which it means cooperating *with* other people – joining hands with them and walking alongside them. Or consider the cooperation of workers and capital owners in production. Labor alone or capital alone will not produce any value. To do so, they must *interact* in production. Benefits from division of labor is a further example. A firm that specializes in printing books will be unproductive unless there is another firm that specializes in typesetting. In this chapter I consider cooperation in this second, interactive sense.

Successful cooperation in this sense requires the solution of two problems. In general, there must be a mechanism for dividing the benefits from cooperation. In cases where universal cooperation is pointless, there must also be a mechanism for deciding who shall be allowed to take a free ride. Either problem can be solved in a decentralized or centralized way. The decentralized mechanism, which is the topic of this chapter, is *bargaining*.[1] In the next, I consider centralized mechanisms.

1 Bargaining may also be required to achieve cooperation in the first, individualistic sense. If there is no point in everybody cleaning up litter from the lawn,

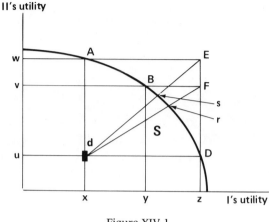

Figure XIV.1

The simplest bargaining problems involve only two persons. They could be the seller and the buyer of a house bargaining over the price, a divorcing couple bargaining over child custody, a union and an employer bargaining over the wage rate or two countries bargaining over how to draw the frontier between them. There can be a number of outcomes, including the one in which the parties fail to reach agreement. Each possible outcome yields some level of utility for each party.

In Fig. XIV.1 the possible utility combinations lie in the set *S*, bounded by the two axes and the curve. If the parties do not reach agreement, their utilities are represented by the disagreement point *d*. Clearly, the parties can do much better if they agree than if they fail to reach agreement. The very multiplicity of possible agreements may, however, prevent any of them from being realized, since each party would like an agreement favoring his interest. (Other details of the figure are explained later.)

Child custody bargaining can be used as an illustration. Here

bargaining may occur over who should be exempt. If some people gain less or suffer more from cooperation, bargaining may take place over the amount of compensation they should get. Everything that is said about bargaining in this chapter applies to such cases too.

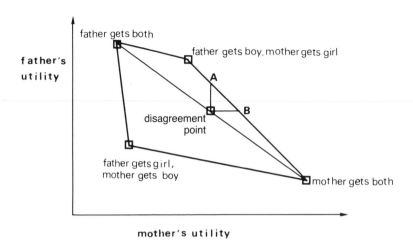

Figure XIV.2

we suppose that the object of bargaining is to get custody of two children, a girl and a boy. There are four basic outcomes: the father gets custody of both children; the mother gets both; the father gets the boy and the mother gets the girl; the father gets the girl and the mother gets the boy. The utility to the parents of these outcomes is represented by the vertices in Fig. XIV.2.

The father is most concerned with getting custody of the boy, whereas the mother would very much like to get custody of both. In addition, there is a number of mixed outcomes, yielding utilities that correspond to the lines between the vertices and to interior points. The mixed outcomes are generated in two ways. They can be lotteries that assign various probabilities to the basic outcomes, or they can be basic outcomes combined with side payments. Custody bargaining is often linked with financial bargaining. The disagreement point is what will happen if the parties go to court. I have supposed that the court is equally likely to award the father or mother custody of both children so that, from their point of view, it is as if the court flipped a coin between these two outcomes. Outcomes in the triangle defined by *A, B* and the disagreement point are better

137

for both parents than a court-imposed solution. Note that one of the basic outcomes is worse for both than the disagreement outcome.

The outcome depends on the *bargaining mechanism* that determines the sequence of proposals and counterproposals. The mechanism can be abstractly thought of as a device that for any pair (S, d) picks out one outcome in S to be realized. The outcome will be somewhere northeast of the disagreement point, since neither party will accept an outcome that gives him or her less than what he or she could get by leaving the bargaining table. Beyond this obvious fact, we have little robust understanding of bargaining. We know how various elements of the situation affect the outcome when other things are kept constant, but that is not the same as being able to say what the outcome will be, all things considered. A brief survey of these partial mechanisms follows.[2]

One element that drives bargainers to agreement is the cost of bargaining. Maintaining a bargaining apparatus, with paid officials or expensive lawyers, is costly. Postponement of agreement is costly in itself if the parties would rather have the benefits earlier than later, as most people would.[3] If the parties were not bargaining over a shrinking pie, they might go on haggling forever. The party with more resources can benefit by deliberate procrastination, knowing that the other would rather reach an unfavorable agreement earlier than a more favorable one later. In divorce bargaining, the husband often forces his wife to accept an unfavorable settlement because she cannot afford to pay a lawyer.

Another element that can force agreement is the use of threats. A union can threaten to strike, hoping that the firm will be deterred by the prospect of losing production and perhaps customers. Betting on the mother's concern for the child's wel-

---

2 Bargaining theory being a somewhat arcane subject, the following exposition is even further removed from rigorous analysis than elsewhere in this book.
3 See chapter V.

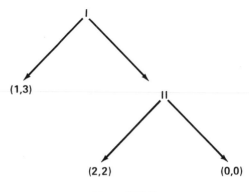

Figure XIV.3

fare, a father could say that he will have nothing to do with his child in the event that the mother gets custody. That threat would not be very credible. If the father is sufficiently concerned to want custody, he would want to see his child if the mother got him. The union's threat could be more credible, if it has some strike funds and if the workers aren't too heavily burdened by mortgage payments and the like. One way of making a threat credible is to precommit oneself to carrying it out, even if it will not be in one's interest to do so when the time arrives.

Social norms can also lend credibility to threats that otherwise would appear empty. Consider the game depicted in Fig. XIV.3. With rational players the outcome of this game will be (2, 2). Player I will move right, anticipating that II will then move left. Although II might threaten to move right if I moves right, the threat is not credible. Assume, however, that II is a "man of honor," known for never making an empty threat or breaking a promise. In that case, the threat to move right if I moves right *is* credible, and I will move left if he is rational. If I, too, is moved by a code of honor that tells him never to be taken advantage of, he will move right and take a loss rather than yield to the threat. As a result, both are worse off than they would have been had I been rational.

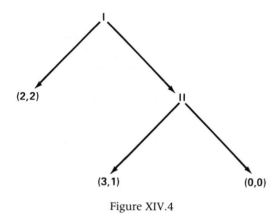

Figure XIV.4

Similar effects may be produced by norms of distribution. Consider Fig. XIV.4. Rational players will converge on (3, 1). Any threat by II to go right will not be credible. Assume, however, that II is moved by an egalitarian norm. In that case, he might be willing to cut off his nose to spite his face: he would rather take nothing than accept the inegalitarian distribution. Knowing this, I will move left, if he is rational. Once again, however, I might also be moved by normative considerations. He might, for instance, believe in a norm of equity that justifies unequal reward for unequal contributions. If I believes himself to have made a greater contribution than II, he too, might take nothing rather than accept the egalitarian distribution.

Agreement is facilitated if one outcome is especially salient. When two countries are bargaining over their common frontier, their task is greatly facilitated if there is a river that goes through the border region. When a country emerging from colonial rule has to choose an official language, the language of the colonial power may be the only one that is acceptable to tribes with widely different dialects. When there are two contenders for the royal throne, a republican regime may be the only thing they can agree on. Equal division of the benefits from cooperation is not always a meaningful concept, but when it is it will often emerge as the focal point of agreement.[4] The force of precedent is also very strong. Even when the relative bargaining power of the parties has been modified, the sheer difficulty of finding a new agreement may keep the old one alive. Sometimes these salient outcomes will compete with each other. One party will say, "Let's split equally," and the other, "Let's do as we did last year."

In a transparent situation, these mechanisms can force an immediate agreement. Although the outcome will be shaped by the credible threats the parties could make, there is no need to carry them out. When the parties sit down to negotiate, the outcome is a foregone conclusion. This does not mean that there is no action, only that it is shifted to the earlier stage at which the parties try to rig the bargaining setup in their favor. To make themselves less vulnerable to threats, the trade union will build up strike funds and the firm will build up inventories. The firm may choose inferior technology, if the best methods of production involve machinery that would make it especially vulnerable to strikes or sabotage. Or the firm might preferentially hire married workers, who are likely to have high mortgage payments and thus be less willing to hold out in a strike. This kind of jockeying for position is wasteful. It is a technique for increasing one's share in the pie at the expense of reducing the size of the pie. Under some circumstances, the workers will want to persuade the firm that they are not going to strike, so that the firm need not engage in these wasteful practices that reduce the total to be shared. To have the desired effect, a promise not to strike would have to be made credible, for instance by not building up a strike fund or by posting a bond.

Usually, however, the bargaining context is far from transparent. The parties have incomplete knowledge about each other, and as a result no agreement may be reached. If the seller believes that the buyer is willing to pay up to $100,000 for the

4 When the object of bargaining is indivisible, even-chance lotteries can serve the same function, except that there is little to prevent the losing party from reneging on the deal.

house, whereas in reality he will pay at most $90,000, no deal may be struck even if the seller would have been prepared to sell it for as little as $80,000. The union may believe that the firm is in better financial shape than it is. This is not just ordinary uncertainty. It is aggravated by the fact that each party has, and knows that the other party has, an incentive to misrepresent its preferences. If the firm says it is in bad shape, the union will easily dismiss it as a routine bargaining move. All divorce lawyers know that fathers often fake interest in custody to force a favorable financial settlement.

A paradoxical aspect of uncertainty is reflected in Groucho Marx's saying: "I wouldn't be a member of a club that would accept me as a member." Sometimes the very fact that a bargain is struck suggests that it was unfavorable. Imagine that in an oriental market you find a carpet that you believe to be a genuine Uphistan, which, in your opinion, would go for five thousand dollars in New York. You can't really afford it, but you don't want to miss the chance of a bargain either. You compromise by offering five hundred dollars, not really believing that the offer will be accepted. Much to your surprise, it is accepted without further haggling. You walk away with the carpet, and an uneasy feeling that it's too good to be true, for would the offer have been accepted if the carpet was genuine? This "winner's curse" arises because the other party's acceptance gives you new information that, had you had it earlier, would have deterred you from making the offer. The moral is: never make an offer that you will regret having made should it be accepted.[5]

Let us shift focus, from discussing whether an agreement will be reached to the question of which agreement will be reached. Often, the outcome of bargaining reflects justice according to Saint Matthew: to him that hath shall be given. Consider the divide-a-thousand-dollar example in chapter XI. Suppose, contrary to what I assumed there, that the two can communicate and haggle over the division. If one is wealthy and the other is

---

5 Solomon's judgment provides another illustration of the way bargaining behavior can reveal preferences.

142

poor, the former will get the lion's share. Since he doesn't really need the money, he can claim, say, eight hundred dollars and say to the other, "Take it or leave it." Since the other needs the money, he will take it. Similarly, people who are averse to risk or myopic will do worse than those who don't mind gambling or waiting.[6]

An unresolved problem concerns the impact of the range of alternatives on the final outcome. Suppose that in Fig. XIV.1 the parties have agreed on the outcome s. Another pair of bargainers face a similar situation, except that there are fewer possible outcomes. Specifically, the set S is truncated by the horizontal line beginning at B so that only outcomes below that line are feasible. It could be a union and a firm bargaining over the length of the working day, with the line representing a legally imposed upper limit. The question is whether the outcome will differ when the set is truncated. One intuitively plausible idea is that it cannot matter whether the parties lose some possible outcomes that they wouldn't have chosen anyway. Since s was the outcome in the larger bargaining problem and remains feasible in the smaller problem, it should be the outcome in the smaller problem too. The outcome should be "independent of irrelevant alternatives."[7] Another plausible idea is that the bargaining power of the parties depends in part on the best outcome they could get. But these ideas contradict each other.

Consider Fig. XIV.1 again. In the full set S, the best II can achieve for himself is w, since I will not accept less than x. Similarly, I cannot hope to get more than z, since II will not accept less than u. In the truncated set, II's best outcome is v. It

---

6 Risk aversion and myopia could be effects of poverty, but they could also arise independently of it.

7 With respect to individual choice this is a quite compelling principle. Suppose that the menu in a restaurant offers three alternatives: beef, chicken and pizza. I decide to order chicken, but when the waiter tells me that there is no more pizza to be had, I change my mind and order beef. Unless the unavailability of pizza tells me something about the likely quality of their chicken, this behavior is irrational. The principle is more controversial in bargaining contexts.

seems plausible that the final outcome should be sensitive to the best outcome the parties can reach. It isn't fair that one party should get almost the maximum he could get, whereas the other must rest content with much less. In the truncated set we would expect the outcome to change in I's favor, since II would get close to his maximum if the outcome remained at *s*. One way of specifying this idea is that the parties' gain, compared with the disagreement point, should be proportional to the maximum amounts they could get. In Fig. XIV.1 the outcome should be *s* in full set and *r* in the truncated set. But this goes against the independence of irrelevant alternatives. The problem is, as I said, unresolved. Perhaps the consensus among scholars is that rational people would not take account of irrelevant alternatives but that actual people do.

Bargaining problems also arise in larger groups. Sometimes it is pointless or even harmful if everybody participates in a co-operative task. Deciding who should take a free ride, and how much they should pay the cooperators, are matters for bargaining. Legal systems can be set up in different ways. It is better for all that there be some law rather than no law, but each particular legal arrangement will benefit some more than others. Bargaining is needed to achieve agreement. Even if all firms in an industry agree on the need to limit production, they must bargain over the production quotas. Trade unions that belong to a central organization must bargain with each other to coordinate their claims before they can bargain with the employers. Parties that enter into a coalition government bargain over who shall get which ministries. The American Constitution was partly an outcome of bargaining. Alexander Hamilton proposed that representation in Congress be based solely on the number of free inhabitants in each state. The Southern states wanted each person, slave or free, to count fully. The outcome was a compromise: each slave was to count as three-fifths of a person.

Bargaining among many persons can easily fail. When there are many mutually beneficial arrangements, with different winners and losers, nobody wants to be the loser. The very multiplicity of cooperative agreements may prevent any of them from being realized. It may be an advantage if one of the bargainers is strong enough to impose his preferred outcome, not by force but simply by telling the others to take it or leave it. Because he is strong it matters less to him whether an agreement is reached, and hence his ultimatum is more credible than it would be if made by one of the others. A biased order is preferable to anarchy. A naturally salient outcome may also allow the parties to agree. Equal representation of all parties in the government or of all states in the Senate can be focal points of agreement.

Bargaining among more than two persons is qualitatively different from bargaining between two persons, in that it allows the formation of *coalitions*. In three-party bargaining, two parties may ally themselves against the third. Nineteenth-century British politics is a classic case. The landowning aristocracy and the industrial capitalists allied themselves against the workers to keep wages down in the mining industry, in which both propertied classes had an interest. Capitalists and workers allied themselves against the landowners to repeal the Corn Laws, which, by protecting British cultivators, made for expensive grain. To gain the support of the workers on that issue, landlords promised their help in the struggle for the ten-hour day. Today, congressional politics and international politics offer numerous instances of coalition building.

Even when no coalition is formed, the possibility that one might be formed can shape the outcome of bargaining. Suppose that a number of people are bargaining over how to distribute the benefits from a cooperative venture and that a certain distribution is proposed. If a smaller coalition in the group can do better for itself by withdrawing from the joint venture to set up its own, smaller venture, the proposed distribution will not be accepted. An acceptable or stable distribution is one that creates no incentive to withdraw for any coalition. Sometimes there are many distributions with this property: further bargaining must then take place to determine which of them shall be realized. Sometimes there are no distributions with this property. An example is

145

a game in which three players are told that they can divide a thousand dollars any way they wish. The method of decision is majority voting. Then, any proposed distribution can be blocked by a coalition. For instance if (50, 50, 0) is proposed, the first and the third persons can block it by proposing (75, 0, 25). That in turn can be blocked by the second and the third proposing (0, 50 50). And so on.

The theory of coalitions is a technically formidable topic, hard to convey by simple examples and intuitive reasoning. I will leave it, therefore, at this point. Fortunately, in a sense, not much is lost, since the theory has few robust results. In another sense, of course, this is most unfortunate, because bargaining and coalition formation are massively important facts of social life.

XV

SOCIAL INSTITUTIONS

INSTITUTIONS keep society from falling apart, provided that there is something to keep institutions from falling apart. On the one hand, institutions shelter us from the destructive consequences of passion and self-interest, but on the other hand, institutions themselves run the risk of being undermined by self-interest, the "rust of societies" as Tocqueville called it. An institution presents two faces, as it were. It seems to act, choose and decide as if it were an individual writ large, but it is also created by and made up of individuals. Each face deserves attention. Although the latter is the more fundamental, I begin with the first and more familiar face.

For this purpose, an institution can be defined as a rule-enforcing mechanism. The rules govern the behavior of a well-defined group of persons, by means of external, formal sanctions. The implied contrast here is to social norms, which enforce rules by external, informal sanctions, and to internalized rules. A policeman may fine me if I litter in the park. If there is no policeman around, other people may glare at me. If there are no other people around, my own conscience may be sufficient deterrence.

Institutions can be private or public, depending on the nature of the sanctions. Private institutions include firms, trade unions, religious organizations and universities. The main sanction at their disposal is expulsion from the group. To make people join, they offer benefits ranging from a wage or a degree to the absolution of sins. Public institutions include Congress, the Securities and Exchange Commission, the Supreme Court and the Board of Education. Their sanctions, backed by the law enforcement system, include subsidies, taxes, fines and imprisonment. The rules enforced include laws, judicial decisions, administrative decrees and executive orders.

Institutions affect us in a number of ways: by forcing or inducing us to act in certain ways; by forcing us to finance activities that we would not otherwise pay for; by enabling us to do things that we could not otherwise do; by making it more difficult for us to do certain things than it would otherwise be; and by changing the context for bargaining among private parties. I shall consider these mechanisms in that order.

Modifying behavior by the use of force is the most striking aspect of institutions. Here "force" means any action intended to make an undesirable practice more costly for those who might be tempted to engage in it. Public institutions, in particular, rely heavily on this means of enforcing their rules. Suppose that the state imposes a tax on liquor to deter people from drinking. This involves two kinds of force. The state uses force against buyers of liquor, by making drinking more costly, but it also uses force against sellers, by making it more costly or risky to sell bootleg liquor. If the purpose of the tax is simply to generate revenue, only the second kind of force is involved. Typically, state revenue is used to finance public goods that would not otherwise be produced, such as basic scientific knowledge or national defense.

Private institutions also use force, and not only by threatening with expulsion. An employers' association may fine member firms that violate its instructions about how far they can go in wage concessions. A firm may punish a shirking worker by denying him tenure or promotion. A church may punish divorce by refusing to be part of a remarriage. The ultimate threat is expulsion, firing or excommunication, but the institution usually has a larger spectrum of sanctions.

Whereas force is intended to make undesirable behavior more costly, inducement works by making a desired behavior less costly. The state gives tax breaks for investment or for donations to charity.[1] It subsidizes firms in peripheral regions or universities that accept students from minority groups. In some countries it supports farmers for cultivating the land, in others for not cultivating it. Often, there is a choice between force and inducement. In modern societies, voting is usually voluntary, sometimes compulsory, but never (to my knowledge) induced by rewards. In classical Athens, by contrast, citizens were paid to attend the assembly. Workers can be forced to join the union if there is a closed shop, or induced by favorable pension and insurance schemes.

Some institutions are set up to enable people to do certain things rather than to deter or to induce them. Laws of contract serve the purpose of enabling people to make binding promises that otherwise would not be credible.[2] Without enforceable contracts, long-term interaction and planning would rest on the fragile bases of honesty and credible threats. It is interesting that there are no institutions that help people make credible commitments to harm themselves or other people. The threat to kill myself unless I get my way could be made credible if there were an institution that was legally allowed and obligated to kill me if I didn't. The threat to take my business away from the firm unless I get a discount could be made credible if there were an institution that was allowed and obligated to sue me for damages if I didn't. It is clearly a good thing that there are no institutions of this kind. It is more puzzling why there are no institutional means to enhance self-control. If I want to quit smoking, I might welcome the opportunity to make an enforceable commitment to pay a thousand dollars to charity in case I resume.

Laws of marriage are enabling: without them, it would not be possible to make a credible, lifelong commitment to another person. Laws of divorce, which are the other side of the coin,

---

1 Indirectly, inducements presuppose force, since the institution can be punished if it fails to deliver the reward.
2 This enabling function also rests on force, since contracts are legally enforceable.

are restricting: they make it difficult to undo the commitment. They do not force people to remain married, but they do create a counterweight to impulsive desires to break up. The most important institutions of this kind are constitutions. The parts of a constitution that make it more difficult to change the constitution than to enact ordinary legislation are analogous to divorce laws. They are not supposed to create an everlasting framework,[3] but to force people to think twice before they change it. Because it is restricting, a constitution is also enabling. Without constitutional guarantees against confiscation of property, for example, long-term economic planning by individuals would be impossible.

Finally, institutions can affect behavior by altering the bargaining context for individuals. In the preceding chapter, I said that since the outcome of bargaining is determined largely by the set of feasible agreements and the disagreement outcome, the parties have an incentive to act strategically on these elements of the situation. Outside parties, such as the state, may also want to modify the situation, for the sake of efficiency or for distributional purposes (as discussed later). The outcome of collective bargaining is affected by legally imposed limits on the working day[4] and by laws requiring or allowing binding arbitration if the parties do not reach agreement. The abolition of debtor's prison had a big impact on private contracting, as did the weakening of the caveat emptor principle.

When institutions affect people's welfare, they can make everybody better off, make some better off at the expense of others or make everybody worse off. Consider a tax imposed on nonfarming activities to subsidize farmers. Initially, the distribution of income is at A in Fig. XV.1.

A percentage tax on income from nonfarming activities will

---

3 As legal scholars say, the constitution is not a suicide pact.
4 If bargaining power is affected by the best outcome the parties can get, as discussed in the preceding chapter, this holds true even if unconstrained bargaining would have led to a working day shorter than the legally imposed limit.

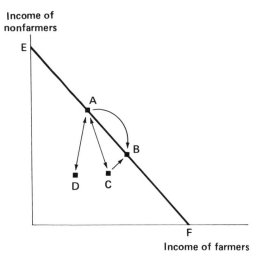

Figure XV.1

usually lead to a loss in total income, since those who are taxed will tend to work less.[5] Since all points at the line *EF* represent income distributions that add up to the same total, the after-transfer distribution must be at some point *C* below this line. At *C* the farmers gain little compared with *A*, whereas the non-farmers lose a great deal. It might even happen that the loss of income of nonfarmers decreases the demand for farm products so much that even farmers end up losing, the final distribution then being *D*. Either outcome, and especially the latter, could easily lead to political pressure to abolish the tax and move back to *A*. Suppose, however, that someone invents a clever form of tax collection that can achieve transfers without loss of production.[6]

5 This may seem obvious, but it isn't, and may in fact be false. When income is taxed, people may work more to maintain the standard of living to which they have become accustomed. Usually, however, this effect is dominated by the tendency to prefer leisure over work when work becomes less remunerative.

6 In theory, this can be achieved by "lump-sum taxation," in which people are assessed a tax that is independent of how much they work and earn. Under this scheme, they have no reason to work less since they retain the full income of each additional hour of work.

This could lead to a move from *C* to *B*. If the device had been thought of in the first place, the move could have been directly from *A* to *B*.

As in this example, institutions can produce five kinds of effects. Some institutional actions are purely *efficient:* they make everybody better off, as in the move from *C* to *B* or from *D* to *A*.[7] Some are purely *redistributive:* they transfer income without any waste, as in the move from *A* to *B*. Other actions achieve redistribution at the cost of some waste, as in the move from *A* to *C*. Still others achieve efficiency[8] at the expense of the redistributive goal, as in the move from *C* to *A*.[9] And some, finally, are purely *destructive,* by making everybody worse off, as in the move from *A* to *D*.

These effects may be intended or unintended. Often, the hoped-for effect is to achieve redistribution, with waste as an unintended side effect. Or the goal is to achieve efficiency, which then turns out to have undesirable redistributive effects. Sometimes the goal is thwarted because the institution does not anticipate the second- and third-order effects of its actions, as illustrated by the failure to anticipate the fall in demand caused by a new tax. When child custody legislation shifted from a maternal presumption rule to the rule that custody should follow the best interests of the child, legislators did not anticipate that the new law would deprive women of a chip they could use in bargaining over the financial settlement. Or the institution might not anticipate that individuals adapt strategically to its

7 There are two notions of efficiency that are easily confused. Changes that make everybody better off are called Pareto improvements, after the Italian economist Pareto. A state in which nobody can be made better off without someone else being made worse off is called Pareto optimal. A Pareto improvement may be a move to a Pareto-optimal state, but need not be so if there is room for further Pareto improvement. A move to a Pareto-optimal state may be a Pareto improvement, but need not be so if someone is made worse off, as in the move from *C* to *A*.
8 That is, Pareto optimality.
9 Of course, this move does achieve redistribution in favor of nonfarmers, an effect that might well be the real motivation behind the tax abolition even if the official motive is the efficiency gain.

actions, as in the failure to anticipate the loss of production caused by a new tax. Another example of the naive belief that the individuals regulated by a law will continue to behave as if they were unregulated was mentioned in the first chapter. If the state makes it obligatory on employers to give tenure to people when they have been employed for two years, many people will be laid off after eighteen months. The end result could be less job security rather than more.

Institutions can make everybody better off by solving collective action problems. A trade union may induce workers to join, and to follow strike orders, by offering special benefits to members. A revolutionary party may force the peasantry to join by threatening them with violence, or induce them by offering educational programs or help with the harvest. To overcome the citizens' propensity to take a free ride, the state can force them to pay taxes and use the revenue to produce public goods. Alternatively, it can force or induce them to act cooperatively, as when firms are fined for polluting or inventors given a state pension.

The collective action problem in Fig. XV.2, characterized by constant benefits and decreasing costs of cooperation, shows how varying degrees of force could make people cooperate. If a large fine is imposed for noncooperative behavior, cooperators always do better than noncooperators. Cooperation is a dominant strategy. With a small fine, both universal cooperation and universal noncooperation are equilibria.[10] Cooperation will be achieved only if people are well informed, so that they can count on each other's cooperation. Once achieved, it would be stable against defectors, but it might be hard to achieve. Similarly, a large inducement would make cooperation a dominant strategy, whereas a small inducement would create one cooperative and one noncooperative equilibrium.

10 In addition, there is a large number of equilibria in which exactly k people cooperate. These are highly unstable, however. If an additional person cooperates, everybody else will, since cooperators now do better than noncooperators. If one person ceases to cooperate, everybody else will, since cooperators now do worse.

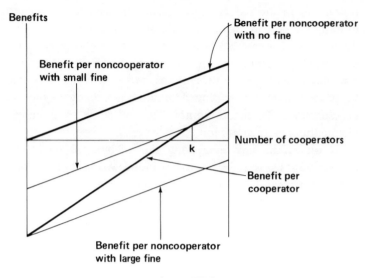

Figure XV.2

I have been saying institutions "do" or "intend" this or that, but strictly speaking this is nonsense. Only individuals can act and intend. If we think of institutions as individuals writ large and forget that institutions are made up of individuals with divergent interests, we can be led hopelessly astray. In particular, the chimeric notions of "the popular will," "the national interest" and "social planning" owe their existence to this confusion.

An institution may be run on dictatorial or on democratic lines. In the former case, the institution does have a "will" and an "interest," although, as we shall see, it may not be easy to execute them. In the latter, more interesting case, it is not clear how the institution's will or interest should be defined. Consider an assembly in which each member is a perfect representative of the interests of his constituency,[11] and suppose that they

11 In reality, of course, no representation is perfect, because the members of the constituency have diverging interests. The choice of a person to represent the interests of the constituency creates exactly the same problems as those discussed later in the text.

have to decide among three proposals. For specificity, think of a municipal assembly that has to choose among building an indoor swimming pool, subsidizing the local symphony orchestra or setting up a golf course. Now, if there is one alternative that everybody thinks is the best, the choice of that option can plausibly be called an expression of the popular will. In politics, however, unanimity is the exception.

It might seem that, when there is a conflict of interest, majority voting will elicit or indeed constitute the popular will. But this proposal doesn't hold water. Suppose there are three blocs in the assembly, of approximately equal size, representing the business community, industrial workers and health and social service professionals. Let us also suppose that, conforming to the stereotype of these groups, they rank the options as follows:

	Businessmen	Workers	Professionals
Golf course	1	2	3
Orchestra	2	3	1
Swimming pool	3	1	2

Suppose that majority voting is taken as an expression of the popular will or the community interest. Then the popular will is that it is better to have a golf course than to subsidize the orchestra, since the businessmen and workers together form a majority with this preference. Similarly, the popular will is that subsidizing the orchestra is better than building a pool, since businessmen and professionals together form a majority with this preference. But the popular will also supports the swimming pool over the golf course, since workers and professionals together have this preference. And this can only mean that the notion of a popular will is incoherent, or that the popular will is itself incoherent, whichever you prefer. If an individual says that he prefers vanilla ice cream to chocolate, chocolate to strawberry and strawberry to vanilla, we would think that he does not

155

understand what it means to prefer something or that he is just mixed up and confused. We would certainly not take his statement as an expression of what he *really* wants. Nor should we take the cyclical majority preferences as an expression of what the community *really* wants.

In the individual case, though, there usually *is* something that a person really wants, although he may have some difficulty in sorting it out. Could we assert the same of the community? One line of argument is that rational discussion among the members of the assembly can overcome the conflict of interest, so that all will come to see that one claim is better grounded than the others. Now, something like this may sometimes be true, but far from always. Time is often short and decisions have to be made before agreement is reached; and sometimes agreement would not be reached even if the discussion went on forever. If people have different ideas about what they would like to do in their leisure time, no amount of discussion will persuade them that music is inherently more valuable than sports.

Another line of argument might seem more promising, namely that majority voting is flawed because it neglects the intensity of preferences. If the music lovers have very strong preferences, while the others don't care much one way or another, it seems that subsidizing the orchestra is the right choice. If we could measure and compare the welfare levels of different persons, we might decide that the popular will lies in the alternative that raises total community welfare by the largest amount. This proposal soon runs into deep philosophical trouble, which need not concern us here since it is in any case totally impracticable. No reliable procedure exists for measuring the intensity of preferences, if only because people might find it in their interest to misrepresent them.

An individual usually knows what he wants; I have argued that a society does not. An individual can usually do what he has decided to do; I shall argue that a society cannot. For the individual, there is no gap between decision and execution, barring weakness of will and physical inability. The transmission machinery from brain to hand has no will or interest of its own to oppose the order from the brain. An institution, by contrast, must rely on individuals with interests of their own. Institutional decisions are easily deflected and distorted by self-serving behavior of the agents who are to carry them out. The most visible and vicious form of opportunism is corruption. Outsiders may bribe officials to shape the rules or violate the rules in their favor. If the agents seek power rather than wealth, they may seek to inflate the bureaucratic machinery and increase their staff beyond what is required by the task. Sometimes they act on their private conception of the institution's interest, disregarding orders from above.

To counteract these tendencies, one may put one's trust in institutional design. Managers are often rewarded by stock bonuses to ensure that their private interest coincides with that of the firm. Institutional goals may be formulated to reduce the scope of fraud and corruption, as when taxes are imposed on land rather than on production. Sometimes jurors, judges and public officials are chosen at random, so that it is more difficult to bribe them. Some public officials are elected rather than appointed, so that they are more accountable for their actions. The Chinese empires made a practice of rotating officials to prevent them from becoming too familiar with the local gentry. There may be rewards for individuals who denounce corrupt practices. One institution may watch over another, and even entrap it by attempted corruption.

These solutions tend to create their own problems. Rotation, election, and random choice of officials work against stability and efficiency. If the point of institutions is to promote efficiency, it makes no sense to tie the hands of officials to prevent them from taking bribes. The methods of tax collection that are least vulnerable to corruption may not give much revenue. If one institution is to watch over another, we must ask: who shall guard the guardians? A system of mutual watching is vulnerable to collusion. An individual who detects a corrupt practice could profit more from blackmailing the corrupt parties than from denouncing them. In general, any mechanism that is supposed to detect and counteract rust formation in the institutional machinery is itself liable to rust.

Although it is hard to prove, I believe that the variation in corruption across countries is explained largely by the degree of public-spiritedness of their officials, not by the cleverness of institutional design. Morality and social norms seem to count for more than enlightened self-interest. Desires matter more than opportunities. This formulation of the problem might be misleading, however. If there are multiple equilibria, accident and history might provide the explanation. Two countries might have the same institutional design and the same mix of individual motivations, and yet one might be ridden by corruption and the other free of it. What seem to be public-spirited motivations may just be public-spirited behavior, motivated by self-interest in an equilibrium in which it pays to be honest. Figure XV.2 illustrates the point. I don't believe this can account for all variation among countries, but I could be wrong.

In any case, it is obvious that institutions are not monolithic entities that can be counted on to transmit and then carry out decisions from the top. Talk about institutions is just shorthand for talk about individuals who interact with one another and with people outside the institutions. Whatever the outcome of the interaction, it must be explained in terms of the motives and the opportunities of these individuals.

XVI

SOCIAL CHANGE

A ROUND 1630 we find Descartes arguing with a friend who believes that a cannon ball reaches its highest velocity some time after leaving the muzzle. The friend's belief is quite natural. When a person starts running, it takes a while before he reaches his maximum speed, after which he eventually runs out of strength. Also, it takes some time before the ball reaches the highest point in its trajectory. The idea of a gradual buildup and then gradual depletion of forces is compelling. It took the genius of Galileo and Descartes to see that *movement is not a process but a state* that will persist indefinitely unless perturbed by external forces. The ball reaches its maximum velocity at the moment of leaving the muzzle and would go on at the same speed in the absence of air resistance and gravity.

Organic metabolism presents another ambiguity. Looked at from close up, the destruction and creation of cells seems to be a process of incessant change, almost chaos. If we step back, however, we see that there is a pattern in the change. New cells of a given kind are being created at the same rate at which old cells are being destroyed,[1] the net result being that the cellular structure as a whole is maintained unchanged. "Plus ça change, plus c'est la même chose." In Norway, there are wooden stave churches built in the twelfth century in which there probably is not a single piece of wood that actually dates from that time, and yet we don't hesitate to say that they are the same churches.

Social change offers analogies to both ambiguities. When eco-

---

1 Unfortunately, this is not true of brain cells (or less true than it is of other cells).

nomic growth occurs at a steady rate of 2 percent per year, does a fall to zero growth represent a change or the cessation of change? Do Chinese dynasty cycles or Latin American coups represent so many changes of political regime, or are they simply the way in which the system maintains itself over time? Is social mobility a form of social change or a form of social metabolism?

In light of earlier chapters the following answer suggests itself: social change is the nonfulfillment of expectations. Subjective surprise, not objective novelty, is the hallmark of social change. In equilibrium, there are no surprises; therefore, social change is an out-of-equilibrium phenomenon. Social change is progressive if outcomes are better than what was anticipated, regressive if worse.[2] The dynasty cycle would, on this conception, be an unbroken chain of changes, or a cycle of regressive and progressive changes. First, the economic environment decays, as irrigation officials divert funds to their own pockets, tax evasion becomes rampant and bandits spring up everywhere. These events occur as the unintended consequences of rational individual adaptations.[3] Then, as the regime runs out of money and legitimacy, it becomes the easy prey of an organized movement to overthrow it. Beginning with a clean slate, the new regime seeks efficiency, justice and the abolition of corruption, but after a while it is once more overtaken by rust and corrosion.

Much of world history exhibits a pattern of political cycles, superimposed on the cycles of day and night, full moon to full moon, seasons, droughts and locusts. No wonder that cyclical theories of history and visions of the eternal return are so attractive. But things can also get steadily worse or steadily better. The trend may be masked by cycles, but not indefinitely. Destruction of the environment is often nearly impossible to undo. Two thousand years ago the land around the Mediterranean, includ-

2 For reasons explained in the preceding chapter, I am being deliberately vague about "better" and "worse." If the change involves winners and losers, it may not be possible to decide whether it corresponds to "the social interest." But sometimes we can tell without much difficulty.

3 Recall from chapter X the link between girl infanticide and banditry.

ing much of the Sahara, was green and fertile. Excessive cultivation and deforestation rendered it barren. Similar ecological disasters occurred on the Chinese plains, in the Oklahoma dust bowl and may be occurring today in the earth's atmosphere.

> Crumbling is not an instant's Act
> A fundamental pause
> Dilapidation processes
> Are organized Decays
>
> 'Tis first a Cobweb on the Soul
> A Cuticle of Dust
> A Borer in the Axis
> An Elemental Rust –
>
> Ruin is formal – Devil's work
> Consecutive and slow –
> Fail in an instant, no man did
> Slipping – is Crash's law.

> (*The Complete Poems
> of Emily Dickinson,* no. 997,
> London: Faber & Faber)

As Marx remarked in a letter, civilization often leaves a desert behind itself. Ecological niches disappear, and sometimes their occupants do too. But there is a counterforce: technical change and, more generally, increasing knowledge. While land lost to the Sahara is never regained, knowledge once acquired is never lost.[4] Throughout history there has been a steady increase in productivity as tools have become more finely tuned to their purpose, animals more productive, grains more resistant to climatic variations and people more skilled. More recently, there has been a change from incremental to discontinuous technical change, as two main obstacles to systematic innovation – myopia and free riding – were removed. Myopia lost its force because, with increasing affluence as the result of incremental innovation, people could afford to think about the future. Nonincremental innovation takes time. Being a case of "one step backward, two steps

---

4 It is easy to think of modifications and exceptions to both statements, but they remain roughly true and important.

161

forward," it requires resources that will allow one to survive in the interim period. Free riding on innovations was eliminated by the institution of patents, which provide the necessary incentive for the would-be inventor.

Technical change has the potential to benefit everybody, but in the short run there are always winners and losers. Some people will lose their economic niche or be displaced by machines. They will have to move elsewhere or starve. As a result of social and geographical mobility, social norms lose their hold on people, largely because people spend a larger proportion of their life with strangers who are not enforcing the norms with the same efficacy. The norm against selling land, prevalent in traditional societies, disappears. The aristocracy pays lip service to the norm against marrrying for money, but violates it in practice. In seventeenth-century England, before the Civil War, the gentry were guided by a norm against entering contested elections. They wanted to be selected, not elected, because losing would be dishonorable. In the latter half of the century, competitive elections came to be accepted, as part of the new, individualistic era in which success, not honor, was what mattered.

When people move from the countryside to the city, face-to-face norms of mutual help or vengeance are dissipated in a sea of anonymity. This normlessness, or *anomie,* is a major cost of progress. Much of the gain from economic progress can be absorbed by the costs of rescuing or policing the losers. Societies that do not assume these costs may find themselves in even more trouble. After a while, new norms may emerge. Horizontal bonds of solidarity come to replace vertical bonds of loyalty. Although selling land is acceptable, there is now a norm against buying votes. Although some norms disappear because one spends more of one's time with strangers, new norms – such as the norm against buying into a cinema queue – appear to regulate relations with strangers.

The strains and stresses of disequilibrium – whether caused by institutional decay, ecological degradation or economic progress – induce different reactions in different groups. The worst off rarely have the resources to do something to improve their fate. The better off do have resources and, unless they are very well off, also the motivation to change things. Tocqueville observed that revolutions do not occur in the worst-off regions of a country or a continent, but in the better-off regions. Feudal oppression was worse in Germany than in France, but the reaction against it came first in France. Standards of living were worse in the French regions than around Paris, which is where the rebellion began. The middle peasantry rather than the poorest form the backbone of peasant rebellions.

Tocqueville also made the closely related point that revolutions occur not when things are getting worse, but when they are improving. Expectations often rise more rapidly than the possibility of satisfying them. In traditional societies, ordinary people adapt to their lot, which is seen as natural, immutable and even desirable. They rationalize their subjection by adopting an attitude toward their rulers that is partly admiration (the Romans adored their emperors as gods), partly denigration ("We wouldn't want their burdens anyway"), partly resignation ("It is not for us") and partly calculation ("Who else would protect us?"). Improvement of conditions and observed social mobility can release people from adaptive preferences. Even if people still believe that the poor will always be with us, they may begin to ask why *they* should be among them. If expectations of individual improvement rise faster than the objective possibilities, the accumulated frustration can trigger collective action.

The actions of the regime will be decisive for the further turn of events. There are two mistakes governments can and do make in a disequilibrium situation: to concede too little or too much. Often, they do the former out of fear of doing the latter. Reforms to meet pressure for abolition of privileges or popular representation will spur popular desires rather than satisfy them, as the Shah of Iran found out too late. Limited freedom of the press is always a dangerous and unstable halfway-house solution. Creating consultative bodies without legislative power is to justify the opposition without satisfying it. Knowing this, many rulers fear to make any concessions at all, thus letting discontent grow beyond bounds until nothing can save them. There are two ways out of this dilemma. One is the democratic system of ongoing conflict resolution, a late development in the process of modernization. The other is for rulers to preempt demands for change – to satisfy claims before they are made. In modern history Bismarck is an outstanding example of one who followed this strategy.[5]

The ability of the regime to resist external pressure depends on its internal health. That, in turn, depends largely on the way it handles its finances. If the regime is engaged in costly warfare, it will be in constant need of funds. If the regime actually runs out of money so that it cannot pay its soldiers, it is lost. If it tries to raise money by short-term expedients, efficacy and legitimacy are eroded. Increasing the tax rate discourages productive investments that could create a larger tax base in the future. The sale of offices undermines the state's ability to act. When the cash nexus replaces authority as the link between superior and subordinate, the state has no limbs to carry out its decisions. At worst, officials sell themselves to the highest bidder; at best, they act according to their private conception of the public interest. The sale of titles devalues the aristocracy by removing any remaining illusions of honor and service. The long-term effect of these acts for short-term gain is loss of legitimacy. Eventually, the regime is no longer seen as acting in the public interest. Badly paid soldiers, recruited from the peasantry, refuse orders to shoot at peasant rebels, and the apparently ironclad regime falls overnight.

Those who gain from progress and would like to gain more may not be powerful enough by themselves to force change. Often, they ally themselves with the losers, the urban proletariat or the poor peasantry. A bargain must be struck that offers some-

---

5 On a lower level the same mechanism is observed when employers make preemptive wage concessions to prevent workers from unionizing.

thing to those who have been displaced by economic progress. To achieve this, the well off must be able to represent their particular interest – the abolition of privilege and royal prerogatives – as being in the interest of all but a small minority. The aristocracy no longer performs any service in return for privilege. The king is squeezing the country rather than strengthening it. The former must be abolished, the latter constrained. "No taxation without representation."

In building a coalition against the old regime, the propertied classes run the risk of playing the sorcerer's apprentice, unleashing forces they cannot control. The poor who spearheaded the change may feel that they did not get their share of the gains from cooperation. Struggles against inequality tend to turn into struggles for equality. The fight against legal privilege turns into criticism of private property. The struggle for more power to parliament turns into a struggle for more equal representation in parliament. The ideological spokesmen for change tend, as do all intellectuals, to go to extremes. For them, a little equality is like being a little pregnant. The revolution moves to the left; monarchy is abolished rather than simply constrained.

This stylized sketch of modernization and revolution is a kind of composite picture of the English revolution of 1640 and the French revolution of 1789. Later revolutions took a different course, partly because they were later and partly because the circumstances differed. In Germany in 1848 or Russia in 1917, the background was not so different, but the reactions of the parties were shaped by these earlier events. The English and French did not know they were making a revolution. Events happened one at a time, unforeseen and surprising, as when a marriage goes to pieces bit by bit. In a marriage of two previously married persons, however, the parties know from the beginning what may happen. Whether the effect is to accelerate the otherwise gradual process of distrust and alienation or to make the spouses act more carefully, it will not be like their first marriage.

For similar reasons, people who know that they are in a

revolutionary situation will be influenced by the scenario of earlier revolutions. In 1848, the German propertied classes were so aware of the risk of entering into an alliance with workers and artisans that their revolution never got off the ground. Instead, there was a return to the earlier regime – or in fact beyond it, to a more entrenched reactionary system. A rational ruler would never want to recreate the prerevolutionary state of affairs, since that by definition is one in which revolutions can occur. Before 1917, the Russian Communists were divided in two groups, one arguing for suspending revolution until capitalism was more fully developed and the other for an immediate grab for power. The latter won out, for good reasons. The former argued that workers should first help capitalists to power and then retreat from the scene to let capitalists create the conditions for a socialist revolution. But in the light of earlier events a rational capitalist class would be very circumspect about entering into an alliance with their future gravediggers.

The Chinese Communists made a similar mistake in 1926–7, thinking they could manipulate the Kuomintang and not understanding that Chiang Kai-shek might figure out what they were up to.[6] After the Shanghai massacre, the Communists changed to a more appropriate stratgegy, based on collective action in the countryside. The success or failure of such peasant-based revolutions depends crucially on the mixes of force and inducement deployed by the revolutionary party and the government. At a given moment, the peasant faces an array of positive and negative sanctions from both sides, together with normative pressure – which could go in either direction – from his peers. In addition, he must figure out how likely it is that the revolutionaries will succeed and, if they come to power, that they will carry out their promise of social justice. Knowing all this ra-

6 One mistake to avoid in politics is to base one's plans on the assumption that the opponent is less rational than oneself. Another mistake is to base one's plans on the assumption that the opponent is just as rational as oneself. As mentioned in chapter II, the opponent's opportunities should figure more centrally than his motivations.

tional revolutionaries will begin in peripheral regions where government forces are weak and the peasants so poor that inducements can be effective. To show that they are incorruptible and not motivated by personal gain, their personal behavior is austere, even ascetic. To demarcate themselves from government forces and from bandits, looting of the peasantry is strictly forbidden. These measures are necessary, but not sufficient, conditions for success. In the end, the outcome depends on the tactical and strategic skills of the two parties – skills that are constrained by rationality but not reducible to it.

The period between 1640 and 1950 was one of massive social upheaval. Today, most people live in societies with stable, reasonably effective institutions, many of which are in the business of *planning* change.[7] Some economies are based wholly on central planning, and all have some scope for government steering and regulation. On this conception, change is not a chain of unintended consequences to which people submit without understanding or control, but a deliberate process of rational improvement. The development of modern social science, together with vastly improved methods for data collection and computation, makes it possible for people to be the masters of their fate, for the first time in human history.

I have little faith in this idea. The ability of institutions to act effectively for large-scale, long-term social change is severely limited, partly for reasons given in the preceding chapter and partly because of the sheer complexity of social causality. Even in planned societies, social change will not embody solutions to problems: it will be the result of a search for solutions. "History is the result of human action, not of human designs." Small-scale tinkering, incremental planning and trial-and-error procedures may seem more promising. Their value is limited, however, by the difficulty of generalizing from small-scale, short-term effects of institutional change to large-scale, long-term consequences.

Since an institution is not like an individual, we have no

7 This is true of India, China, the Soviet Union, the United States and Eastern and Western Europe.

guarantee that its intentions will remain stable over time, even assuming that individual intentions remain unchanged. A plan that depends on sustained, unwavering adherence to one set of policies could be undermined by a new majority undoing a decision made by an earlier one. Moreover, the plan, even if consistently adhered to at the top of the political system, might not be faithfully executed at the lower levels. These problems were discussed in the preceding chapter. Here I consider some additional difficulties.

To decide upon a plan, a planner must have two kinds of information. He must know the current state of the economy, and he must have a causal theory that relates earlier states to later states. The current state is represented by the desires and opportunities of the agents in the economy – consumer tastes and productive capacities. Such information is always hard to come by. For one thing, it may not be in the interest of people to reveal their preferences and capacities truthfully. Consumers will not report their true evaluation of a public good if the purpose is to tax them proportionally. Under central planning, firms have an incentive to underreport their capacity so as to make it easier to fulfill the plan. For another, the economic agents may not even know their preferences and capacities. Households may not be able to tell how their consumption plans would be affected by a change in prices. Firms may be unaware of the full range of productive techniques at their disposal. They know the technique they are currently using, not the ones they might adopt under hypothetical circumstances.

The greatest obstacle to planning arises from the lack of reliable theories of society. What we have is a toolbox of mechanisms, not a set of laws. We cannot predict how rational people behave under conditions of uncertainty or multiple equilibria, nor whether their behavior will be governed by rationality or by social norms. Even more fundamentally, we cannot predict how preferences and norms might themselves come to change as a result of policy reforms. We cannot predict technical change. As

Humphrey Lyttleton said about a similar problem, "If I knew where jazz was going I'd be there already." Developments in the international economy and in military relations among states are an additional source of uncertainty and indeterminacy, as are the unforeseen ecological changes that are constantly thwarting the best-laid plans.

This is a gloomy picture, but are things really so bad? Couldn't we realize the plan step by step, retreating and replanning when necessary? Small-scale experiments could precede large-scale implementation. For an example, consider the idea of introducing cooperative ownership as the mandatory form of organizing firms, thus doing away with private property. This form may seem good on paper, but one would be wary of imposing it just on the basis of theoretical considerations. Instead, one might set up some firms of this type to see whether their actual behavior confirmed what theory predicts. If it did, the next step would be to extend the scope of the reform, for instance by making it mandatory in firms below a certain size. If that, too, were successful, the threshold size might be gradually increased up to the point, if any, at which cooperatives became less efficient than capitalist firms.

There are several problems, however, with this attractive proposal. Institutional change might have very different consequences when implemented in the small and in the large. There are at least four reasons the performance of isolated cooperatives might not be a good indicator of what an all-cooperative economy would be like. There could be a bias due to positive or negative self-selection. Isolated cooperatives might attract exceptionally motivated workers – or excessively adventurous, risk-loving individuals. There could be a bias due to positive or negative discrimination. The cooperatives might receive support from outside groups that were ideologically committed to the reform, but they might also be less favorably treated by banks, suppliers and customers than their capitalist counterparts. There could be a bias due to positive or negative externalities. The cooperative might benefit from innovations made by their capitalist counterparts or suffer from a loss of their workers to capitalist firms.[8] Finally, there could be a bias due to adaptive or counteradaptive preference formation. Some workers might shy away from cooperatives because their preferences have adapted to the capitalist environment. Others might be attracted to them because they are attracted by doing something that few others are doing.

Of these, the mechanisms that favor the isolated cooperative create no problems. As the scope of the reforms increases, there will come a point at which these advantages lose their force. At that point one could have a stable mix of different types of firms. The mechanisms that work against the isolated cooperative are much more disturbing. If the results are negative, the planner would scrap the reform and conclude that the capitalist mode of ownership is, after all, superior. In doing so, he might miss an opportunity. An all-cooperative economy could be superior, perhaps by a great deal, to an all-capitalist one, even if isolated cooperatives do worse than capitalist firms in a capitalist environment.

Couldn't the planner experiment on a large scale, to get around this problem? Apart from other, obvious objections, the proposal suffers from a fatal flaw. Large changes have many effects, often working in opposite directions, affecting desires no less than opportunities. It will take a long time – perhaps centuries – before the dust has settled and the equilibrium properties of the new system can be ascertained. It would require an improbable degree of patience and endurance to wait it out, especially since it would always be contestable whether any bad properties are just transitional phenomena or part of the new equilibrium. The only thing that could motivate people to suffer

8 This argument must be spelled out. Even in a fully capitalist economy, firms face the possibility that they might not recover the cost of on-the-job training of their workers if they are enticed away by other firms. Cooperatives are even worse placed, however. By virtue of the more extensive interaction and participation in decision making, their members receive more extensive on-the-job training.

the transition costs would be perceiving the reform to be a matter of basic justice, not economic efficiency.[9] In that case, however, we are not talking any longer about social planning, but about a social movement for reform.

9 The transition to political democracy was in part supported by a conviction of this kind.

BIBLIOGRAPHICAL ESSAY

I MECHANISMS

THE issues of scientific explanation discussed here are explored in many books on the philosophy of science. Carl Hempel's classic *Aspects of Scientific Explanation* (New York: Free Press, 1965) remains a fine starting point. A good study of causation is Tom Beauchamp and Alexander Rosenberg's *Hume and the Problem of Causation* (New York: Oxford University Press, 1981). Neither deals specifically with explanation in the social sciences. On that issue the reader might turn to Philippe van Parijs, *Evolutionary Explanation in the Social Sciences* (Totowa, N.J.: Rowman & Littlefield, 1981) or to my *Explaining Technical Change* (Cambridge University Press, 1983). A critical discussion of "storytelling" in biology can be found in Philip Kitcher, *Vaulting Ambition* (Cambridge, Mass.: MIT Press, 1985). Many of the points Kitcher makes also apply to storytelling in the social sciences. The view that progress in the social sciences consists in knowledge of ever-more mechanisms rather than in ever-better theories is expounded in Paul Veyne, *Writing History* (Middletown, Conn.: Wesleyan University Press, 1984).

II DESIRES AND OPPORTUNITIES

The economist's view that choices can be explained by the preferences of the agents and the opportunities they face can be found in any textbook on microeconomics. The philosopher's view that choices can be explained by the desires and beliefs of the agents has been expounded by Donald Davidson in a num-

173

ber of influential essays, collected in his *Essays on Actions and Events* (New York: Oxford University Press, 1980). The view that people have essentially similar preferences and differ only in the opportunities facing them is argued in George Stigler and Gary Becker, "De gustibus non est disputandum," *American Economic Review* 67 (1977): 67–90. The view that preferences (even if they differ across people) don't matter because the constraints are so tight that no room is left for choice is sometimes espoused by Marxists and members of the French Structuralist school. The influence of desires on opportunities and of opportunities on desires is argued in, respectively, chapter II of my *Ulysses and the Sirens* (rev. ed., Cambridge University Press, 1984) and chapter III of my *Sour Grapes* (Cambridge University Press, 1983). The idea that fewer opportunities may be better than more is brilliantly stated in chapter 5 of Thomas Schelling, *The Strategy of Conflict* (Cambridge, Mass.: Harvard University Press, 1960) for the case of strategic interaction. References to the case of weakness of will are given below (under Myopia and Foresight).

III RATIONAL CHOICE

Introductory expositions of the theory of rational choice can be found in the articles by Gary Becker and John Harsanyi in Jon Elster, ed., *Rational Choice* (Oxford: Blackwell Publisher, 1986). A superb exposition of the relation between preferences, utility and action is R. Duncan Luce and Howard Raiffa's *Games and Decisions* (New York: Wiley, 1957). Here the reader will also find clear and accessible statements of game theory and the theory of choice under risk. A more recent (and more difficult) introduction to game theory is James Friedman's *Game Theory with Applications to Economics* (New York: Oxford University Press, 1986). The idea that concern with ends–means rationality can be self-defeating is elaborated in chapter II of my *Sour Grapes*. Problems of rational-belief formation and rational collection of information are discussed in many of the essays collected

174

in Peter Diamond and Michael Rotschild, eds., *Uncertainty in Economics* (New York: Academic Press, 1979).

IV WHEN RATIONALITY FAILS

Indeterminacy of choice due to brute uncertainty is discussed in chapter 13 of Luce and Raiffa, *Games and Decisions,* and in the contributions by Isaac Levi and by Peter Gärdenfors and Nils-Eric Sahlin to Peter Gärdenfors and Nils-Eric Sahlin, eds., *Decision, Probability and Utility* (Cambridge University Press, 1988). Levi's *Hard Choices* (Cambridge University Press, 1986) is mandatory reading for those with an interest in this issue. I do not know of any general discussions of indeterminacy due to strategic uncertainty, but perusal of pp. 90–4 in Luce and Raiffa, *Games and Decisions,* and of pp. 137–43 in Anatol Rapoport, *Two Person Game Theory* (Ann Arbor: University of Michigan Press, 1966), will suggest the nature of the difficulty. The theory of satisficing is developed by Herbert Simon and expounded in the essays collected in vol. 2 of his *Models of Rounded Rationality* (Cambridge, Mass.: MIT Press, 1982). Weakness of will is discussed at length in Robert Dunn, *The Possibility of Weakness of Will* (Indianapolis, Ind.: Hackett, 1987). Irrational belief formation by "hot" or motivational mechanisms is discussed in David Pears, *Motivated Irrationality* (New York: Oxford University Press, 1984) and in Leon Festinger, *A Theory of Cognitive Dissonance* (Stanford, Calif.: Stanford University Press, 1957). Irrational belief formation by "cool" mechanisms is discussed by Richard Nisbett and Lee Ross, *Human Inference: Strategies and Shortcomings of Social Judgment* (Englewood Cliffs, N.J.: Prentice Hall, 1980) and in many of the essays collected in Daniel Kahneman, Paul Slovic and Amos Tversky, eds., *Judgment under Uncertainty* (Cambridge University Press, 1982).

V MYOPIA AND FORESIGHT

An exposition of the standard theory of time discounting (Fig. V.2.A) is Tjalling Koopmans, "Stationary ordinal utility and impatience," *Econometrica* 28 (1960): 287–309. A famous discussion of the nonstandard case (Fig. V.2.B) is R. H. Strotz, "Myopia and inconsistency in dynamic utility maximization," *Review of Economic Studies* 23 (1955–6): 165–80. The discussion in the text of the nonstandard case draws heavily on the writings of George Ainslie, most recently summarized in his "Beyond microeconomics," in J. Elster, ed., *The Multiple Self* (Cambridge University Press, 1986). Discussions of self-control include chapters 3 and 4 in Thomas Schelling, *Choice and Consequence,* and chapter II of my *Ulysses and the Sirens.*

VI SELFISHNESS AND ALTRUISM

A number of discussions of this issue are found in Jane Mansbridge, ed., *Against Self-Interest* (University of Chicago Press, forthcoming). A survey of altruism in economic life is David Collard's *Altruism and the Economy* (Oxford: Robertson, 1978). Some approaches from social psychology are found in Valerian Derlega and Janusz Grzelak, eds., *Cooperation and Helping Behavior* (New York: Academic Press, 1982). An unorthodox theory of the relationship between these two motivations is proposed by Howard Margolis, *Selfishness, Altruism and Rationality* (Cambridge University Press, 1982). The distinction among the various altruist motivations is further explored in chapter 5 of my *Cement of Society* (Cambridge University Press, 1989). Problems of paternalism are discussed in Rolf Sartorius, ed., *Paternalism* (Minneapolis: University of Minnesota Press, 1983), and in Donald van DeVeer, *Paternalistic Intervention* (Princeton, N.J.: Princeton University Press, 1986).

VII EMOTIONS

A useful collection of writings on the emotions is Amélie Rorty, ed., *Explaining Emotions* (Berkeley and Los Angeles: University of California Press, 1980). A survey of philosophical theories of the emotions is William Lyons's *Emotions* (Cambridge University Press, 1980). Psychological aspects are explored in Carroll E. Izard, Jerome Kagan and Robert B. Zajonc, eds., *Emotions, Cognition and Behavior* (Cambridge University Press, 1984). The typology of emotions sketched in the text draws on my "Sadder but wiser? Rationality and the emotions," *Social Science Information* 24 (1985): 375–406. The contrast between self-realization and consumption draws on Richard Solomon and John Corbit, "An opponent-process theory of motivation," *Psychological Reviews* 81 (1974): 119–45. The question of the rationality of the emotions is explored in Ronald de Sousa, *Rationality and the Emotions* (Cambridge, Mass.: MIT Press, 1987). The suggestion that emotions both give meaning to life and distort our cognitions has some experimental support in Lauren Alloy and Lyn Abrahamson, "Judgments of contingency in depressed and non-depressed students," *Journal of Experimental Psychology: General* 10 (1979): 441–85, and in Peter M. Lewisohn, Walter Mischel, William Chaplin and Russell Barton, "Social competence and depression," *Journal of Abnormal Psychology* (89) (1980): 203–12. For a discussion of envy see Helmut Schoeck, *Envy* (Indianapolis, Ind.: Liberty Press, 1987). Two good case studies of the emotions are Robert Levy, *The Tahitians* (University of Chicago Press, 1973), and Malcolm Budd, *Music and the Emotions* (London: Routledge & Kegan Paul, 1985).

VIII NATURAL AND SOCIAL SELECTION

Good accounts of the working of natural selection are Elliott Sober's *The Nature of Selection* (Cambridge, Mass.: MIT Press, 1984) and Philip Kitcher's *Vaulting Ambition* (Cambridge, Mass.: MIT Press, 1985). Good discussions of social selection are Richard Nelson and Sidney Winter's *An Evolutionary Theory of Economic Change* (Cambridge, Mass.: Harvard University Press, 1982) and Michael Faia's *Dynamic Functionalism* (Cambridge University Press, 1986).

IX REINFORCEMENT

An excellent textbook is John Staddon, *Adaptive Behavior and Learning* (Cambridge University Press, 1983). It may usefully be read together with John Staddon, ed., *Limits to Action: The Allocation of Individual Behavior* (New York: Academic Press, 1980), and John Dupré, ed., *The Latest on the Best* (Cambridge, Mass.: MIT Press, 1987). On the relevance of reinforcement theory to human behavior, see Richard Herrnstein, "A behaviorial alternative to utility maximization," in S. Maital, ed., *Applied Behavioral Economics* (London: Wheatsheaf Books, 1988), and William Vaughan and Richard Herrnstein, "Stability, melioration, and natural selection," in L. Green and J. Kagel, eds., *Advances in Behavioral Economics,* vol. 1 (Norwood, N.J.: Ablex, 1987).

X UNINTENDED CONSEQUENCES

A classic study of this phenomenon is Robert Merton, "The unanticipated consequences of social action," *American Sociological Review* 1 (1936): 894–904. A good modern analysis is Raymond Boudon, *The Unintended Consequences of Social Action* (New York: St. Martin's Press, 1981). I explore some logical aspects of the problem in chapter 5 of my *Logic and Society* (New York: Wiley, 1978). The economic theory of externalities is explained, with some technicalities, in chapter 3 of Partha Dasgupta and Geoffrey Heal, *Economic Theory and Exhaustible Resources* (Cambridge University Press, 1979) and, somewhat less technically, in William Baumol, *Welfare Economics and the Theory of the State* (2d ed., London: Bell, 1965). The problem of explaining actions through their unintended consequences is addressed in chapters VIII and IX of G. A. Cohen, *Karl Marx's Theory of History* (New York: Oxford University Press, 1978), in chapter 3 of my *Explaining Technical Change* (Cambridge University Press, 1983), in Philippe van Parijs, *Evolutionary Explanation in the Social Sciences* (Totowa, N.J.: Rowman & Littlefield, 1981), and in Arthur Stinchcombe, "Merton's theory of social structure," in

Lewis Coser, ed., *The Idea of Social Structure: Papers in Honor of Robert Merton* (San Diego, Calif.: Harcourt, Brace, Jovanovich, 1974).

XI EQUILIBRIUM

An accessible introduction to this topic can be found in chapter 1 of Werner Hildebrand and A. P. Kirman, *Introduction to Equilibrium Analysis* (Amsterdam: North-Holland, 1976). The rest of the book is more difficult. The nature and the role of the equilibrium concept in economics are explored in depth in John Harsanyi, *Rational Behavior and Bargaining Equilibrium in Games and Social Situations* (Cambridge University Press, 1977) and in John Harsanyi and Reinhart Selten, *A General Theory of Equilibrium Selection in Games* (Cambridge, Mass.: MIT Press, 1988). A thought-provoking application to more general issues is Robert Sugden's *The Economics of Rights, Co-operation and Welfare* (Oxford: Blackwell Publisher, 1986). The notion of a convention equilibrium derives from David Lewis, *Convention* (Cambridge, Mass.: Harvard University Press, 1969), drawing on chapter 2 of Thomas Schelling, *The Strategy of Conflict* (Cambridge, Mass.: Harvard University Press, 1960). The issue of rational versus adaptive expectations is addressed, by defenders of respectively the former and the latter, in David Begg, *The Rational Expectations Revolution in Macroeconomics* (Oxford: Allan, 1982) and in Hashem Pesaran, *The Limits to Rational Expectations* (Oxford: Blackwell Publisher, 1987).

XII SOCIAL NORMS

This chapter draws heavily on chapter 3 of my *Cement of Society* (Cambridge University Press, 1989). A useful empirical survey is Robert Edgerton's *Rules, Exceptions and the Social Order* (Berkeley and Los Angeles, University of California Press, 1985). An alternative approach, with more emphasis on the cognitive role of norms, is Francesca Cancian's *What Are Norms?* (Cambridge University Press, 1975). An evolutionary account of norms is offered in Robert Frank, *Passions within Reason* (New York: Norton, 1988). Good analyses of the closely related phenomenon of trust can be found in Diego Gambetta, ed., *Trust* (Oxford: Blackwell Publisher, 1988). Codes of honor are discussed in R. MacMullen, *Corruption and the Decline of Rome* (New Haven, Conn.: Yale University Press, 1988), and in Christopher Boehm, *Blood Revenge* (Lawrence: University Press of Kansas, 1984), to name but a few. Norms regulating the role of money are discussed in chapter 4 of Michael Walzer, *Spheres of Justice* (New York: Basic Books, 1983). Norms of consumption are discussed at length in Pierre Bourdieu, *Distinction* (Cambridge, Mass.: Harvard University Press, 1986). The norm against rate busting is discussed in Stephen Jones, *The Economics of Conformism* (Oxford: Blackwell Publisher, 1984).

XIII COLLECTIVE ACTION

Two standard books on the problem of collective action are Mancur Olson's *The Logic of Collective Action* (Cambridge, Mass.: Harvard University Press, 1963) and Russell Hardin's *Collective action* (Baltimore, Md.: Johns Hopkins University Press, 1982). The diagrammatic exposition used in the text comes from Thomas Schelling, *Micromotives and Macrobehavior* (New York: Norton, 1978). Cooperation in iterated collective action problems is studied in Robert Axelrod, *The Evolution of Cooperation* (New York: Basic Books, 1984) and in Michael Taylor, *The Possibility of Cooperation* (Cambridge University Press, 1987). Fine-grained investigations into the conditions that promote or hinder collective action are Pamela Oliver, Gerald Marwell and Ruy Teixeira, "A theory of the critical mass. I. Interdependence, group heterogeneity, and the production of collective action," *American Journal of Sociology* 91 (1985): 522–56, and Gerald Marwell, Pamela Oliver and Ralph Prahl, "Social networks and collective action: A Theory of the critical mass III," *American Journal of Sociology* 94 (1988): 502–34. Empirical studies include Samuel Popkin, *The*

Rational Peasant (Berkeley and Los Angeles, University of California Press, 1979), and John Bowman, *Capitalist Collective Action* (Cambridge University Press, 1989).

XIV BARGAINING

Two classic and accessible studies of bargaining, with emphasis on the ploys and stratagems used by real-life bargainers, are Thomas Schelling, *The Strategy of Conflict* (Cambridge, Mass.: Harvard University Press, 1960) and Howard Raiffa, *The Art and Science of Negotiation* (Cambridge, Mass.: Harvard University Press, 1982). An exposition of the formal theories of bargaining that dominated the field before 1980, and remain widely used, is Alvin Roth, *Axiomatic Theories of Bargaining* (New York: Springer, 1979). Expositions of a more recent approach, due largely to Ariel Rubinstein, can be found in Alvin Roth, ed., *Game-Theoretic Models of Bargaining* (Cambridge University Press, 1985), and in Ken Binmore and Partha Dasgupta, eds., *The Economics of Bargaining* (Oxford: Blackwell Publisher, 1986). A (relatively) accessible statement of the modern theory of bargaining is that of John Sutton, "Non-cooperative bargaining theory: An introduction," *Review of Economic Studies* 53 (1986): 709–24.

XV SOCIAL INSTITUTIONS

Recent discussions of the spontaneous emergence of institutions as solutions to problems of coordination and collective action include Andrew Schotter, *The Economic Theory of Social Institutions* (Cambridge University Press, 1981) and Robert Sugden, *The Economics of Rights, Co-operation and Welfare* (Oxford: Blackwell Publisher, 1986). Writers who emphasize the role of institutions in reducing the costs of transaction among members of society include Douglass North, *Structure and Change in Economic History* (New York: Norton, 1981) and Oliver Williamson, *The Economic Institutions of Capitalism* (New York: Free Press, 1985). The role of constitutions is discussed in the contributions to Jon Elster and

Rune Slagstad, eds., *Constitutionalism and Democracy* (Cambridge University Press, 1988). The problem of defining the popular will is discussed in Kenneth Arrow, *Social Choice and Individual Values* (2d ed., New York: Wiley, 1963), and in William Riker, *Liberalism Against Populism* (San Francisco: Freeman, 1982). The causes and consequences of corruption are surveyed in Arnold Heidenheimer, Michael Johnston and Victor LeVine, eds., *Political Corruption* (New Brunswick, N.J.: Transaction Books, 1989).

XVI SOCIAL CHANGE

Information about the Chinese dynasty cycle can be found in Edwin Reischauer and John Fairbank, *East Asia: The Great Tradition* (London: Allen & Unwin, 1960). For a comparative perspective one may consult Carlo M. Cipolla, ed., *The Economic Decline of Empires* (London: Methuen, 1970). Two outstanding studies of the European revolutions of the seventeenth and eighteenth centuries are Lawrence Stone, *The Causes of the English Revolution* (London: Routledge & Kegan Paul, 1972) and Alexis de Tocqueville, *The Old Regime and the French Revolution* (many editions). Good books on the German, Russian and Chinese revolutions include Theodore Hamerow, *Restoration, Revolution, Reaction: Economics and Politics in Germany, 1815–71* (Princeton, N.J.: Princeton University Press, 1966), Leon Trotsky, *The History of the Russian Revolution* (London: Pluto Press, 1977), and Yung-fa Chen, *Making Revolution: The Communist Movement in Eastern and Central China, 1937–45* (Berkeley and Los Angeles, University of California Press, 1986). The comments on planned social change draw heavily on chapter IV of my *Solomonic Judgements* (Cambridge University Press, 1989). A similarly skeptical analysis can be found in Friedrich Hayek, *Law, Legislation and Liberty* (3 vols., London: Routledge & Kegan Paul, 1978).

INDEX

DATE DUE

NOV 2 1 1990		
R. Emmett		
JAN 0 4 1998		